D1106800

DEAR SIR:

YOU CUR

by
SHANDY HILL

WHITMORE PUBLISHING CO.
Philadelphia

Library of Congress Catalog Card Number: 69-17521
Manufactured in the United States of America

CONTENTS

CHAPTER   Page

1	A STIFF BACKBONE	1
2	THE ROAD TO JUSTICE	4
3	HOW IT STARTED	17
4	A GOOD BEGINNING	32
5	BARK HEARD 'ROUND THE NATION	41
6	MR. JAMES P. CROW, ESQ.	50
7	HAS THE NEGRO MADE PROGRESS?	58
8	ALL EQUAL HERE	62
9	A CITY MADE OVER	65
10	SUFFER THE LITTLE ONES	77
11	FOR THE LEAST OF THESE	85
12	POLICE REFORMATION	88
13	A DECISION FROM HIGH	94
14	SCHOOL FOR JOURNALISTS	101
15	HIS FAVORITE DAY	106
16	THE LUCK OF THE PRESENT	111
17	NOTHING NEW UNDER THE SUN	119
18	SAVING AN INDUSTRY	128
19	WHO'S MORE COMPLACENT?	134
20	ENFORCING THE LAW	139
21	THEY'RE WELCOMED HOME	146
22	MYSTERY NEVER DISCLOSED	151
23	CAN'T WIN 'EM ALL	156
24	FLINGS AT THE WHITE HOUSE	158
25	PURELY LOCAL	165
26	CRITICS ALWAYS PRESENT	175
27	DEAR SIR, YOU CUR	182
28	POTTSTOWN ON PARADE	186
29	EPILOGUE	190

ACKNOWLEDGEMENTS

The author acknowledges with thanks the cooperation of William B. Sweetland, vice president of Peerless Publications, Inc. (publisher of the Pottstown Mercury), for permitting him access to the files and use of material of The Mercury. (Copyright, June 16, 1959, to November 24, 1965, Pottstown Daily News Publishing Company).

Also to:

—Jack B. Polish, counsel for Pyramid Productions, Inc., New York, for use of the first 61 words of "The Big Story" radio script of July 9, 1954 (Copyright), as an introduction to the autobiography.

—*Time Magazine,* to quote from the article, "Warning to Pirates" (July 19, 1963). Copyright, Time, Inc., 1963.

—The American Society of Newspaper Editors, Gene Giancarlo, executive secretary, for permission to use excerpts of the proceedings of the Society, copyright 1961 and 1964.

—*Pottstown on Parade,* J. Paul Jones, editor, for permission to reprint the 1952 article, "His Business is News."

—The Bell Telephone Company of Pennsylvania, John Brady, public relations manager, for permission to reprint the article, "We Salute," from the 1962 Pennsylvania Newspaper Publishers Association Bulletin.

Chapter 1

A STIFF BACKBONE

The script called it a "zoom," a crescendo of attention-getting sounds. The "zoom" faded, and was succeeded by soft background music, then the mellifluous baritone of the National Broadcasting Company's announcer:

"You're on a small-town paper, Shandy Hill, the kind of paper William Allen White called 'the backbone of American journalism,' " the introduction of "The Big Story" said.

"And you've got quite a name for yourself around here for sticking out your neck when a good long stretch of spine is needed.

"This is the story as it actually happened. Shandy Hill's story as he actually lived it."

*   *   *   *   *

"The Big Story," as the title indicated, was a radio program of the early 1950's that glamorized noteworthy stories of America's newspapers, large and small. Frequently it had to do with crime. Sometimes it recounted exposés, sometimes holocausts. It featured meritorious work, "as faithfully reported by the men and women of the great American newspapers."

Shandy Hill's big story, first done on radio and then two and one-half years later on television, told the story of how this "small-town newspaper" campaigned for years to obtain the freedom of a man convicted of murder.

Convinced a man prominent in civic life had been convicted on circumstantial evidence in the garroting of a divorcee, the paper joined with a private investigator to obtain new evidence, in a bid for a new trial. Turned down on this plea, it continued its fight before the Pennsylvania Board of Pardons. There, with the help of talented lawyers, a big-city newspaper and the "Court of Last Resort," its fight was won. The prisoner was freed after four and a half years, his sentence of ten to twenty years commuted.

When "The Big Story" on radio, and later the television play, "The Case of the Open Window," blanketed the nation, it may have been the first time listeners and viewers had ever heard of The Pottstown Mercury. Possibly not many remembered the name. It was a small-town paper, and its voice wasn't heard too far away from home base.

But Pottstown, Pennsylvania, and the entire nation were to know the name in 36 years of crusading and campaigning by Shandy Hill, called flatteringly by some in his own profession a "legendary figure." Others used the well-worn cliche, "a newspaperman's newspaperman." He made his newspaper one of the most honored in the nation.

Fortunately, radio and television did not present Shandy Hill as a Hollywood-style newspaperman who solved his case through one blinding flash of inspiration, but as one who stuck to the fight through years of determined, often discouraging digging.

For although Shandy Hill normally sought the anonymity of his profession, he gleaned many honors in the doing.

While he practically remade a city of 25,000, his paper was known mostly as a defender of the underdog, and a crusader for the right. In the process, it became a proving ground for young newspapermen. His graduates into metropolitan fields attested to the thoroughness of his school of journalism.

He presided at the founding of a "new" newspaper in the depths of the Depression. So vigorous was his editorial success that it quickly begot business success, and The Pottstown Mercury went on to win many battles on the field of journalistic honor. While his blows for honesty and integrity in law enforcement and government were never deadened, while his attacks on anything considered faulty were uncushioned, his paper never was sued for libel.

2

He became known as a "controversial" figure—although none who introduced him that way gave a concise definition of the word. Possibly it was because he thrived on controversy.

This is the story as Shandy Hill lived it, not only "The Big Story," but the day-to-day story of many triumphs, some failures, some lighthearted incidents, in a field to which he devoted his entire professional career of 45 years.

And this is the story as Shandy Hill wrote it, told in the third person because, Shandy Hill explains, "I have always had an intolerable dislike for the perpendicular pronoun, both the personal 'I' and the editorial 'we.' "

This, then, is the Shandy Hill story.

Chapter 2

THE ROAD TO JUSTICE

A newspaper's conscience is bared when it fights, often against great odds, for justice. The Mercury, a small-town newspaper, couldn't still its conscience when it felt a conviction of murder was unjust and based on insufficient and circumstantial evidence.

The newspaper's duty to protect the innocent is a challenge no newspaperman worth his salt can reject. Shandy Hill picked up the gauntlet and waged the battle in the highest court of the state, to the Board of Pardons, and finally obtained freedom for the wrongly accused.

He learned that the road to justice is rutted with frustrations, with obstacles erected by those insisting "the case is closed." But that road also is smoothed—by those strongly believing in justice. When those believers include brilliant legal minds, justice eventually wills out.

So it was with the Green murder case, which national radio and television dramatized four and a half years after The Mercury obtained the convicted man's freedom.

*　*　*　*　*

It was a lurid case. A pretty 27-year-old divorcee was found strangled in her apartment. A Pottstonian prominent in civic affairs was charged with having murdered her. Police said he snuffed out her life by twisting a gaily colored scarf around her neck.

He admitted to adultery. He had "run around" with the woman for some months, but he hadn't murdered her, he insisted. He was hundreds of miles away on a deer-hunting trip when the murder occurred. He "discovered" the body, he said, when he returned from that trip to keep a tryst, and was so shocked he told only his wife of the ghastly discovery.

The suspect's wife, parttime parish secretary of a church with the largest congregation in Pottstown, believed his story and remained steadfastly on his side. Over the years, she depleted all their savings, she sold their home and a lot they owned to establish her husband's innocence.

Mrs. Catherine O'Meara, mother of the murdered woman, also was convinced the accused was not guilty. She offered a $500 reward to anyone coming forward with evidence leading to the conviction of the killer. The garroted woman's sister worked steadfastly to obtain freedom for the convicted. These three women were the best of friends over the tortuous years.

The police couldn't make up their minds about what to do with the case, and they seemed to disregard evidence that pointed away from their original suspect—the boyfriend. But they finally placed the murder charge, and it stuck.

But an incredible number of inconsistencies arose. The accused went free on bail, an infrequent occurrence for a murder suspect in Pennsylvania jurisprudence. After he was tried and convicted, he was released again on bail, also said to have been unprecedented in the court's jurisdiction. He resumed his daily occupation, and for almost a year, took his accustomed place in society while lawyers argued for new trials.

The State Supreme Court rejected a new trial plea after lower-court requests also were turned down, but the chief justice wrote a precedent-shattering dissent after declaring in open court that "this case never should have gone to a jury."

* * * * *

The "murderer" seemed doomed to languish in jail for at least ten years, when a brilliant criminal lawyer volunteered to plead with the Board of Pardons for justice, serving without fee likely at the suggestion of the chief justice himself, who had told the convicted man's wife that he knew a lawyer who might gain her husband's freedom, but qualified his statement with the assertion she probably could not afford his services.

5

Such was the background of the case that sent Gerald C. Wentzel to jail, and might have sent him to the electric chair.

How The Pottstown Mercury fought to protect its story, while fighting for four and a half years to free Wentzel, is a story of reportorial maneuvering that often frustrated the Philadelphia and New York metropolitan papers.

The "metropolitans" were stymied by this small-town paper from the time Wentzel was charged formally with murder until his commutation of sentence was handed down, and The Mercury scored a good clean beat on an interview while the metropolitan newspapermen were beating on penitentiary gates.

Yet the story began for The Mercury with nothing but chagrin.

*   *   *   *   *

In the middle of a Monday afternoon, a telephone call came to Shandy Hill from a former Mercury employee, Joseph Harper, then a Philadelphia Inquirer deskman.

"How's that murder coming along up your way?" asked Harper, who had been a courthouse correspondent and close to the coroner's office.

"We've got no murder here," Hill replied. "What are you talking about?"

"You sure have," Harper advised. "Better check."

And so, from Philadelphia came the tip on a murder four blocks from the newspaper office.

No staffers were on duty then, so Hill himself ran to the murder scene. Detectives from the district attorney's office already had completed their preliminary investigation. They had taken photographs of the murder scene, and had dusted for fingerprints. The body was released to a morgue.

Pottstown Police Chief James A. Laughead still was interviewing residents in the vicinity.

"Why didn't you give me a tip on this?" Hill complained. "I had to get the news from Philadelphia."

The policeman brushed the newsman off with an irritated reply:

"I was too busy running down here myself to call anybody," he said.

* * * * *

Mrs. Miriam Green's body was lying flat on its back on her bed. The body was covered with a camel's hair coat. Except for a pair of blue socks, she was nude.

She had been strangled by what police at first said was a scarf or a towel. A door was open, and December's cool air kept the apartment house heater running, because the thermostat was in her bedroom. When a neighbor found her upstairs apartment too warm, she went to Mrs. Green's apartment to find out why the heater kept running. An open door yielded to her knock, and the body was discovered.

A local physician determined that Mrs. Green had been dead at least 24 hours. Police questioned George W. Green, from whom she had obtained a divorce only a week before, and Wentzel, whose photograph was in her wallet. Both suspects were released.

The story simmered for almost a month, and finally disappeared from the paper entirely because there were no new developments. Early in January, however, Wentzel was questioned again, and then jailed. "Inside" information came to Hill that Wentzel was to be charged with murder the next day—at a noon hearing.

This was a convenient time for the metropolitan papers, because they could flood Pottstown with afternoon editions to take the edge off the story. The Mercury, a morning paper, would have to be content with a second-day story.

It was Pottstown's story, Hill told Mayor William A. Griffith, asking him to delay the hearing until it was too late for the afternoon papers. Word already had leaked that some afternoon papers were ready to "replate" or make over Page One for extra editions. They, too, had the same tip that Wentzel would be held for murder.

Wentzel was brought to Pottstown from a county jail for a

7

12:45 P.M. hearing. But delay followed delay. Metropolitan newspapermen scoured the town in taxicabs, trying to find Chief Laughead. They tried downtown restaurants, they tried his home, while Mayor Griffith and Hill sat in the chief executive's front office.

Once in a while, the mayor asked, "All right now, Shandy?" and the newsman replied, "Let's wait a few minutes more."

It was almost 4—too late for the afternoon metropolitans to do anything with the hearing—when Justice of the Peace Richard H. Cadmus and Chief Laughead appeared. The visiting newspapermen had lost a lot of their enthusiasm for the hearing by that time.

Laughead read the charge (the justice of the peace was blind). Lawyer Wellington H. Rosenberry, Jr., Wentzel's counsel, sat silently beside his client. Cadmus softly announced Wentzel would be held for court.

Edging over toward Hill, Laughead grinned broadly.

"You know where I was when those reporters were banging on my house door?" he asked, as if to apologize for his original failure to disclose the murder.

"You know where I was? I was hiding in the cellarway!"

* * * * *

Wentzel was freed on bail. Within two weeks, he was indicted by a grand jury, but he continued on the job as a diecaster at a local industrial plant.

Early in April, almost four months after Mrs. Green's body was found, Wentzel went on trial. During four days of testimony, he steadfastly maintained his innocence, but he was found guilty of second-degree murder and sentenced to ten to twenty years in the penitentiary.

"I was guilty of adultery," he said repeatedly, "but not murder."

So stubbornly did he stick to this assertion that some observers mistook his behavior for arrogance. He defiantly declared he had been on a hunting trip "with the boys" from Friday to Sunday. Yes, it was true he visited Miriam's apartment Sunday night, but she was dead when he arrived. He tiptoed out of her apartment and failed to close the door tightly.

Why hadn't he told police about this immediately? He was afraid.

Where was his key to the apartment? He confessed his peccadilloes to his wife the day after his discovery, he said. She told him to throw the key into a river.

*   *   *   *   *

His lawyer asked for a new trial. Montgomery County Court rejected the plea.

Next, his counsel prepared to take his case to the state Supreme Court.

In the meantime, The Mercury began working with Paul Kleinspehn, a private detective, to obtain "new" evidence.

A "break" came when the undertaker who prepared Miriam Green's body for burial hinted that livor mortis was so far advanced that the corpse must have lain on its back for more than the 24 hours the original testimony showed. Discoloration of the back was so apparent that days might have been required for blood to drain so completely from the upper portion of the body, then seep through blood vessels into the tissue to blacken the skin, the mortician believed.

Kleinsphen obtained a new statement from the Pottstown physician who had pronounced Mrs. Green dead. The doctor said he might have erred when he set the time of death at 24 hours before the body was discovered. Death might have occurred 48 hours or longer before discovery of the body, he now declared.

Hill and Kleinspehn asked District Attorney E. Arnold Forrest to reopen the case on the basis of this new evidence Forrest, later to become president judge of the county, fixed a cold eye on his interviewers and flatly intoned, "The case is closed."

9

The district attorney thus rejected the very medical opinion that was to become the most impressive testimony before the Pennsylvania Board of Pardons but given by a more imposing and prominently known authority.

Attorney Rosenberry made an impassioned plea before the State Supreme Court for a new trial. His argument that Wentzel had been convicted on circumstantial evidence impressed Chief Justice George P. Maxey.

"The Wentzel case never should have gone to a jury," the chief justice commented during the hearing.

Nevertheless, the Supreme Court denied a new trial by a vote of 4-to-3. Here again occurred another action unprecedented in Pennsylvania jurisprudence. For the first time within memory, a chief justice wrote a stinging minority report.

Judge Maxey made a detailed analysis of the testimony of Dr. John C. Simpson, coroner's physician, who placed the time of Mrs. Green's death as 24 hours before the body was found. Maxey concluded, "The evidence convinces me beyond a reasonable doubt that Mrs. Green was killed sometime on the night of Friday, December 6."

If the chief justice was right, Wentzel's alibi that he was on a hunting trip, hundreds of miles from Pottstown, from Friday night until Sunday night, might hold up.

* * * * *

There was to be no new trial, but Mrs. Evelyn Wentzel, wife of the accused, and Mrs. Evelyn Eckenroth, sister of the slain woman, never relinquished their hopes for a reprieve. They were told about the Court of Last Resort, a public-service feature of Argosy magazine that often aided the innocently jailed.

They felt they were grasping at straws, but they wrote Argosy. Tom Smith, former warden of Washington state prison and then a fulltime Court of Last Resort worker, came to Pottstown to interview the principals. After speaking to

10

The Mercury, and to lawyers and judges in Harrisburg, he pledged the magazine's aid.

Then, out of a clear sky, Hill received a telephone call from Thomas J. McBride, a Philadelphia lawyer who had won many colorful criminal cases and whose name often was in the headlines.

"Shandy, I have a new angle in the Wentzel case, and I plan to present it to the Board of Pardons. The difficulty is that Earl Selby, city editor of The Philadelphia Bulletin, has the story and wants to use it on Sunday. I told him that was your story—but I'd like to have your permission for him to publish it. The publicity may be helpful to Wentzel."

The decision wasn't hard to make, even though The Mercury had slaved alone for many years to gain Wentzel's freedom. Words and headlines were the ammunition, depicting the truth as seen. But if The Bulletin were to smash the story on Page One, where the governor, every politician, every member of the Board of Pardons could see it, possibly Wentzel could be helped.

"I'll go along," Hill told McBride.

And so, although The Mercury was to be beaten by 24 hours, The Mercury cooperated. For the fact is, The Mercury hadn't heard the full story up to this time.

* * * * *

The story was fantastic. A Pottstown soldier, serving with the Army in Germany, had confessed to the murder of Miriam Green. At the moment, he was in the federal penitentiary at Lewisburg, Penna., where he had been transferred from Europe, after having been found guilty of armed robbery of a German taxi driver.

He had "confessed," the Army said, in May, 1950, but the story hadn't leaked until November of that year.

Where McBride got the tip was conjectural. Hill believed it came out of Harrisburg, probably from someone close to the state courts.

A new Montgomery County district attorney, J. Stroud Weber, was in office. Prison authorities—possibly military authorities—had given him a transcript of the "confession," but he sat on it. Confronted by newsmen, Weber admitted having the statement, but said he hadn't read it.

McBride and Rosenberry quickly characterized Weber's actions as "a reproach to the whole concept of justice."

Weber apologized. He said he thought he had furnished copies of the "confession" to McBride and Rosenberry, but he never had.

Weber was assailed editorially by The Mercury for his lack of cooperation with the defense. Indignantly pointing to this editorial, he finally resolved to travel to Lewisburg to interview the "confessor."

The editorial got action, and the Bulletin's Sunday story brought the Wentzel case to light once more, even though the confession was repudiated by the ex-Army man.

McBride did not relent. He carried his fight to the Board of Pardons in May, 1951. His "after-discovery" evidence showed that Mrs. Green had been murdered on Friday, not Sunday. He presented statements from nationally known medico-legal authorities that Mrs. Green must have been dead 24 to 60 hours before Wentzel's Sunday-night visit. Dr. Lemoyne Snyder, of Lansing, Michigan, an expert associated with the Court of Last Resort, has produced the "new" medical evidence.

McBride also argued that the soldier, although he had repudiated his murder confession, did admit he had visited Mrs. Green's apartment that fatal Friday night—and said he had found her dead.

*　*　*　*　*

Prospects looked bright for Wentzel, and Hill laid his lines for an exclusive story. His friendship with Eastern State Penitentiary authorities paid off. Hill asked them to give him an exclusive break on an interview when Wentzel was freed.

INTERVIEW to bolster the successful campaign to have a convicted murderer's sentence commuted was this between Gerald Wentzel, left, and Shandy Hill. The Pennsylvania Pardon Board handed the freedom edict after years of Mercury campaigning.

The story came more quickly than anticipated. Several weeks later, on May 20, 1951, Hill, at home, received a telephone message from the penitentiary.

"The word's in, Shandy," he was told. "Come right down and you can get your story."

Hill telephoned the office. The pardon story hadn't come over the news association wire from the capital in Harrisburg as yet. He told them of his plans, and quickly drove 20 miles to the "pen."

He sat alone in the guards' room for a few moments, before Wentzel came striding up a corridor, head erect, pace measured, face devoid of expression. A guard opened the door, and Wentzel strode in, extended his hand and sighed, "It's good to see you. It's good to see you."

Authorities told Hill he could have five minutes. The interview lasted for an hour, while newspapers from all over the East literally were knocking on the penitentiary's gates. Jail officials said they knew nothing about the Board of Pardons decision!

Prayers and faith did it, Wentzel said. Tears welled in his eyes, but otherwise he was expressionless. He didn't smile. He was as grim as when he was on the witness stand.

"I feel no bitterness to those who put me in jail," he said. "I prayed to be forgiven because I forgave others."

The Mercury that day told how the sentence of ten to twenty years was commuted. Attorney Rosenberry explained, "Commutation of maximum sentence is unusual. I can't recall another case like it in recent years."

Commutation meant Wentzel was to undergo no restrictions of parole, but the conviction of second-degree murder stayed on his records.

*　　*　　*　　*　　*

Argosy, in its August, 1951, issue, reprinted an editorial from the May 24 issue of The Mercury, dealing with Wentzel's fight for freedom.

Henry Steeger, the magazine publisher, prefaced the reprinting by writing: "We'd like to invite Shandy Hill to tell you the story because he tells it so well. He's one of the most brilliant editors in the country and his paper, The Pottstown Mercury, is one of our most vigorous and alert newspapers."

In a four-page photographic summary of the case, Argosy cited "The Court of Last Resort's indispensable allies": Evelyn Wentzel, who worked four years to vindicate her husband; W. H. Rosenberry, Wentzel's attorney; Thomas D. McBride, who volunteered his aid in Wentzel's appeals; Katie O'Meara and Evelyn Eckenroth, the slain woman's mother and sister respectively; The Pottstown Mercury and Shandy Hill, who "courageously championed Wentzel's appeal for justice."

The editorial, "The Fight for Freedom Won," appeared the day after Wentzel was released. In it, Hill said: "Gerald Wentzel breathed in some fresh air for the first time in more than three years, yesterday. He stepped out of the Eastern penitentiary, and thus ended a long struggle of his family, his friends, and some persons he didn't even know. It was a struggle to see an injustice undone. Seldom did a case attract so much legal help from persons who regarded it as a cause célèbre."

Then the editorial went on to congratulate Attorney William H. Rosenberry, Jr., "who worked so many hours in so many years to prove his client innocent. Aligned with Rosenberry was the brilliant Thomas D. McBride, Philadelphia lawyer, who displayed such brilliance at Board of Pardons hearings.

"Certainly much praise must go to Tom Smith, investigator for The Court of Last Resort, a humane organization subsidized by Argosy magazine," The Mercury editorial continued. "He used all his experience as a penologist, all his knowledge of crime detection, to uncover evidence that convinced the pardon board of Wentzel's innocence. Smith was one of the most colorful figures in the late stages of the

Wentzel cases. His personal investigation led Dr. LeMoyne Snyder, of Lansing, Michigan, to write a concise opinion that Miriam Green could not have been killed at the time the Commonwealth [of Pennsylvania] contended. That time element was most important, for an alibi was established for the convicted man when the State set the murder time.

"The Court of Last Resort performed a notable public service."

Nowhere in the editorial was there a word of praise for The Mercury for its behind-the scenes work.

*   *   *   *   *

After a short vacation with his wife, Wentzel took his place back in society. Pottstown accepted him as if there had been no interruption of his civic life. He went back to work, trying to recoup the $70,000 he and his wife had spent on his defense. His civic club elected him a district governship.

Yes, there were reminders, constant reminders, he said, of the almost four years he spent in jail. But he never hid his background. He got along on face value.

Reminders? It is unbelievable, but in September, 1966, almost 20 years after the trial, he received a bill for $700 for county court costs!

Chapter 3

HOW IT STARTED

Ralph H. Spare, secretary of the Pottstown Chamber of Commerce, looked up patronizingly at his two young visitors. They had asked him for figures on employment, bank resources, population and the like.

"What do you want this for?" he inquired, smiling.

"We are going to start a newspaper in Pottstown," said 22-year-old William M. Hiester, of Reading.

"Why, we already have a newspaper in Pottstown," Spare protested.

It was so like the old chestnut—"What do I want with a book? I already have one"—that Hiester and Shandy Hill couldn't help exchanging grins and knowing glances.

For Shandy Hill was Spare's other visitor. At 30, he was sports editor of the Reading Times, and Hiester was his assistant.

Much more affluent than his friend and editor, Hiester was the grandson of George F. Baer, millionaire coal mine and railroad magnate in Reading. Hiester's mother, Mary, was Baer's daughter, and had inherited millions.

Hiester had the wherewithal; Hill had the enthusiasm and knowhow.

Spare had nothing but skepticism. His answers to the young men's questions were depressing. It was 1930, the depth of the Depression. Little to inspire optimism was on the horizon, and the prospect of a new industry, injecting new capital into Pottstown's economy—a second newspaper—didn't seem to impress Spare.

Nor was anyone else agog at what these youngsters felt was earth-shaking news. Word of a new newspaper generated little more than curiosity. Some sidewalk superintendents watched

FIRST ISSUE of the Pottstown Mercury was published September 29, 1931. The front page of this Volume 1, Number 1, featured a congratulatory letter from the White House from President Herbert Hoover and an editorial outlining the paper's goals and ambitions. It contained 26 pages.

construction of a printing press pit with knowing nods, and predicted, "I'll give 'em six months." Some predictions were not even that charitable.

An army of local unemployed applied for jobs, but no printers or pressmen or newsmen were among them. Help had to be recruited from distant points, but this, too, was easy to find. Any number of excellent artisans was available because the Depression had depleted newspaper composing rooms.

Spare's pessimism didn't deter the establishment of the newspaper. Neither did the skepticism of the unemployed who watched construction go on in a building which once housed the morgue of a furniture dealer-mortician. Hiester got married, and left on a long honeymoon trip. But Hill remained to superintend the uncrating of hundreds of boxes of assorted machinery, and watch it assembled magically into mechanical wonders.

A summer sped by, printers and pressmen and newsmen and advertising solicitors were hired, and the first issue of The Pottstown Mercury made its debut on the afternoon of September 29, 1931.

The lead editorial, which began on Page One and continued to the editorial page read, in part:

"A new bearer of tidings greets you today. Every evening henceforth, The Mercury will come to your home, bringing with it the latest intelligence from the far corners of the world; not only from High Street, but from Piccadilly Circus, Der Lindenstrasse, Avenue de l'Opera, the Rialto and other centers of activity.

"As The Mercury today makes its bow, a period of preliminary survey of almost a year is ended. Almost 12 months ago, William M. Hiester, owner of The Mercury, decided there was a field for a modern newspaper in Pottstown. Encouraged by a host of Pottstown's leading citizens, and activated by a desire to aggrandize the town in which he received his boyhood education, Hiester slowly began the establishment of a newspaper enterprise he hopes will fill a longfelt need in this community.

CO-FOUNDERS of the Pottstown Mercury were Shandy Hill (left) and William M. Hiester, who started the afternoon daily during the depth of the 1931 depression, but who soon guided it to a pinnacle among small town newspapers

"Today we are able to present to the public a concise report of the world's happenings. We realize this is not a finished product. It is young. It will grow, and with its growth, we hope, will come perfection."

* * * * *

There was more to the editorial. The last paragraphs explained some of the background of the paper's founding.

It didn't explain then, or any other time, how many hours the two young journalists had toiled over plans for a new newspaper or how much courage it took to gamble a lot of money on such an enterprise, without mention of defeat, of loss, of opposition, of failure. Not until many years later, when The Mercury was a success, were newspaper people generous enough to say, with faint praise, "It took lots of guts to start a newspaper in the Depression."

The 12-month preparatory survey didn't disclose many bright prospects. Pottstown was run down at the heels, as was most of America at the time.

The young journalists were certain that the old, established Pottstown newspaper, The News, could be eclipsed. The News, founded in 1887, was in the morning field. It had a paid circulation of little more than 9,000 in a 19,000-population town.

The two strangers didn't consider The News a "modern" newspaper. They might be excused for youthful overenthusiasm if they ill-manneredly mentioned in the opening editorial that they would give Pottstown "a modern newspaper" to "fill a long felt need in this community."

But they were right, and they matched modernity against old-fashionedness. It wasn't much of a fight. The News capitulated, and sold out to Hiester less than two years later.

* * * * *

The old, established morning News of 1931 had been an eight-to-sixteen-page newspaper. It had few features. It had

21

only one comic, "Maggie and Jiggs." It employed no social editor or sports editor until it got wind of the plans for a new paper. It had an Associated Press franchise, but received only a 20-minute "pony" report of telephoned news from Philadelphia. It was not promotional in any way. It clipped most of its state, national and world news from Philadelphia papers that came to Pottstown by train at 1 A.M. The News had no deadlines to speak of, and could wait for this copy. Most of the News circulation beyond the center of town was delivered by mail; much of this delivery by mailman took place after 11 A.M. and some in the afternoon.

The News was gray. It lacked luster. It rarely reproduced photographs. It had no editorial opinion to speak of, and its editorial column was just that—one column! Most of this editorial "opinion" was clipped from other papers. Rarely did editorials touch on local issues.

Page One consisted mainly of social news, such as weddings, and long accounts of dreary civic club dinners. The paper never campaigned for local improvements. Its chief fault was lack of backbone, and the community's poobahs and its subscribers practically dictated policy. When someone commanded, "You can't publish that!" the item was not published. Subscribers walked into the plant and demanded, "I want this on Page One," and the item got on Page One.

Most of the staff was aging. Management had grown old, complacent and lethargic. The advertising staff consisted of one man and he was of retirement age. The paper was owned by an estate that seemed to have lost direct control over the management; the estate couldn't seem to rid itself of what it felt was a millstone around its neck. One of its most ludicrous attempts to erase an employee was to feature a series of stories that pointed up his alleged misbehavior in a nearby seashore resort.

The News was in a modern building, erected in 1926. A complaint frequently heard on the inside was that too much money was spent to erect a monument. It had splendor, all right, but wasn't very functional, except in the mechanical department. It had enough equipment to put out a finely printed paper, with eight linotype machines, a 32-page press and other excellent adjuncts. But it had no editorial direction to speak of, and no writers of better than hack style.

The Mercury flung against its competitor a competent young news staff, although its mechanical equipment could not match its adversary's.

Hiester spent less than $200,000 to equip The Mercury plant; a lot of money then, but there was no extravagance. The 24-page Duplex tubular press, second- or third-hand, purchased from Phoenix, Arizona, had been built in 1907, but it worked like a charm.

There were four linotype machines originally. Sufficient type was cast by working day and night—and even enlisting the aid of News printers for after-hours work. Stereotype equipment came with the press. There was a scattering of advertising banks, an Elrod casting machine. The editorial department was furnished with desks and chairs picked up locally.

The Mercury recruited its editorial staff from local persons, except for one experienced reporter from Reading. It began with a social news editor, a city editor, a telegraph editor, a sports editor and three news writers. All the deskmen pitched in with news writing contributions. So did Shandy Hill.

There was an advertising staff, a classified ad solicitor, and other functionaries The News couldn't match.

But the thing that attracted most attention was the news wire service. The Mercury had United Press (then an afternoon news service) and two teletype machines (one was a spare). This was something new for Pottstown. Local people flocked into the news room to marvel at this wonder of the age!

The Mercury had Central Press for features and King Features for syndicated comics. It bought an auxiliary feature service from the Seattle Star.

The Mercury devoted a full page to editorials and features, including local editorials. It had a daily editorial cartoon, a New York column by James Aswell, a woman's column by movie star Gladys Glad and a medical column by Dr. Logan Clendenning.

The Mercury gave Pottstown a complete comic page, also unknown to the News. There were five eight-column strips, including Muggs McGinnis, Frank Merriwell, Etta Kett, High Pressure Pete and Big Sister, all from King Features. There was one panel, "The Old Home Town," a feature that lived until the 1960's.

There was a separate sports section, a social department and two "county" pages for news from the nearby large communities of Boyertown and Royersford-Spring City. Each community had a bureau manned by writer-advertising-circulation men.

The new afternoon daily depended heavily on human interest and feature stories. It crusaded and campaigned. It promoted heavily. The town took to the new product.

* * * * *

It was a great day for the two young men that September 29. The Mercury, eight columns wide and 22 inches deep, had so much advertising copy that the 24-page press lacked the capacity to handle it. So two sections were printed, for a total of 26 pages. The sections were collated by hand.

For two weeks, The Mercury was distributed free in Pottstown borough and environs, and then went out for paid subscribers only.

The first issue had almost 50 percent advertising, or more than 2,000 column-inches.

The second issue, the next day, had a disappointing total of 59 inches of advertising.

Wondering what had happened to this local support, spoken about in the opening editorial, the two tyros went to the merchants and asked them why they weren't supporting the new paper.

A few months before, they all had sat in the front row, applauding the arrival of the new publication, because they figured a second paper could end the high advertising rates of the established paper.

Now the merchants were silent. Or else they would say, "Oh, the paper's all right," implying, "Go out and get yourself a reputation. Then we'll be with you."

The Mercury's national advertising representative was more precise about his promises: "Get 5,000 circulation and you'll get on the Chesterfield cigarette list." This meant a big hurdle. Chesterfield advertising was lucrative, and it would draw other advertisers.

The Mercury did that, quickly, with the aid of steady promotion and good journalism.

The paper kept the public informed of the progress by Page One boxes. Within a month, The Mercury had a paid circulation of 3,370. By the end of November, the sworn paid circulation was 4,590, and by December 22, 1931, the magic figure of 5,000 was surpassed. This was less than three months after the new paper saw the light of day.

The most circulation the old established newspaper, The News, had ever reached in its 50 years was 9,100.

*　　*　　*　　*　　*

The Mercury was not without competitive struggles.

Its almost instant popularity and its rapid circulation rise led owners of the old established News to make overtures. Hiester accepted the proposals and purchased The News, its building and assets, its goodwill and circulation, in February, 1933. The papers were merged, and a combined evening newspaper was published that March. There was no morning edition.

Accustomed to a morning newspaper for a half century, Pottstown raised a terrific storm. The town still wanted its news in the morning, but for economic reasons, The Mercury remained in the afternoon field. In addition, The Mercury had to terminate the services of many long-term News employees, in order to be loyal to its own workers who had struggled to establish the paper in lean years.

This built resentment.

The two factors resulted in more profitless years, and only by great publishing acumen and skill was The Mercury able to emerge as a champion in its field.

First, the dismissed News employees sold stock locally and established a morning paper, The Herald, within a year after the merger of The News and Mercury. The Mercury, anticipating a struggle, switched to the morning field to meet its adversary on common ground and mollify the complaining readers. But the battle dragged on and the Herald died only after almost six years of competition. It died of anemia. It lacked the monetary resources and journalistic skills to combat successfully the now established Mercury.

One of the wisest decisions The Mercury made was to reject an offer to buy and then kill the Herald when it was on its deathbed. Such a move certainly would have antagonized many more local persons, who hadn't much love, as it was, for the carpetbaggers from Reading who already had disrupted their reading lives.

*   *   *   *   *

One battle was won, but The Mercury was not able to relax for long. The Norristown Times-Herald, the county-seat evening daily, turned envious eyes on the Pottstown market, and after the second World War began printing a "Pottstown edition." The Times-Herald opened a Pottstown office directly across the street from The Mercury. It housed several editorial staffers, who telephoned their news 18 miles away to Norristown. The Times-Herald "Pottstown edition" consisted of only a Page One with Pottstown news, perhaps some continued stories on page two.

The Norristown experiment lasted 13 weeks. Then it, too, died. Insiders said Norristown had lost $100,000 on the venture.

The Mercury, in its opening statement, promised it would be "frank and fearless in all matters, especially in which Pottstown was a vital interest. It will advocate strenuously economy and honesty in its government. It will never assume a vacillating attitude."

Early training on a crusading newspaper led Hill, to use the well-worn cliché, to believe it was the newspaperman's duty to comfort the afflicted and afflict the comfortable.

Hill frankly told civic groups that The Mercury was to be more than a mirror to reflect the day's events. It would be the people's guardian, the defender of truth, the watchdog of the community. Don't look for a newspaper that will drift along with the tide, he warned, or merely be a messenger for the politicians, or for any establishment.

"If you want that kind of paper, The Mercury is not the paper for you," he told them. It was the way he got a tag of "controversial," which invariably was included by every program chairman in every introduction speech.

The Mercury generated the inevitable ill feeling that harasses all editors who conduct fighting newspapers. There were many doubts and suspicions about this intense interest in the community, some charges that The Mercury sought power, some notions that the paper "wanted to run the town." Naturally, The Mercury was the butt of all these charges, but it didn't allow the comments to cause too much worry.

In a talk to a civic club, Hill once asked:

"Did we keep the faith? In some of our campaigns for a better community, we were threatened by the removal of advertising patronage by certain industrialists because we rid the community of slot machines and cut into the revenue of the country club.

"From a Pottstown minister, I was promised a 'biff on the nose' because we refused to wage a crusade against Sunday sports, which he himself would not wage from his pulpit.

"There were attempts at bribes. We were offered several

27

thousands of dollars from a social club to stop writing about those slot machines. A labor leader threatened to throw up a picket line around The Mercury because we injured his feelings."

The Mercury afflicted the comfortable in all strata of society because it felt it was its duty to challenge everything that appeared faulty, unsound or at variance with the public interest.

And it put out a complete paper every day, without aping the big city papers. The Mercury was strictly a local newspaper, and before long earned a reputation as one of the greatest of small-town papers.

* * * * *

It didn't take long to convince the public the paper would print all the news without fear or favor.

In its third issue, The Mercury editorialized in favor of the borough-manager form of government, in which a professional administrator would operate the municipality's business. The Mercury didn't win this crusade easily. It took 14 years of constant flailing away before, in 1945, Pottstown's first manager was appointed.

Long neglect or lack of journalistic enterprise by the old established Pottstown newspaper had given municipal officials a feeling of confidence that they could transact the public's business anywhere except in the open. Officials probably could be forgiven, because many didn't know the people had a right to know, and the newspaper had been content to print what officials wanted it to print. There had been no investigative reporting; the newspaper never asked "Why?"

So secret or star-chamber sessions were not unusual. Municipal committees often met in private homes, where food and drink were available. The Board of Health had a gay old time each month, The Mercury was told, when it was entertained in its chairman's recreation room. School directors, especially, were likely to hold their policy making sessions behind closed doors.

The Mercury smoked out these secret meetings. Adroit reporting revealed what happened in these "secret" sessions, including quotations. Possibly only portions of the discussions were reported, but even their incompleteness was damning. These revelations—always with the written reminders that events took place in secret—became so annoying to some elected officials that they eventually decided to let The Mercury report all meetings, including committee meetings, which certainly were beyond the newspaper's right.

Pottstown officials got the word early. But some municipal and school bodies outside the borough's boundaries were astonished when they learned The Mercury planned to extend this coverage, with full quotes. Elected officials whose loose tongues wagged incessantly for years found these complete quotes didn't look as well in print as they sounded in the governmental halls. But they learned, as Pottstown councilmen learned, the quotes were fairly accurate. For in Pottstown, when lawmakers declared, "I didn't say that!" the borough manager was likely to play back tape recordings to show that memory was shorter than the printed word.

Some suburban government officials literally quaked when they saw Mercury reporters approaching. But many admitted later that the reporters' presence put a damper on irresponsible diversions and increased efficiency.

One of these bodies did outfox a staffer once when the elected officials conducted a meeting in Pennsylvania Dutch, a corruption of German and English still spoken by natives in the local "Dutch Country." The neophyte reporter came back red-eared, apologizing that he couldn't understand. While the editors managed to suppress a smile, the tyro was told it wouldn't happen again. And it didn't.

*　*　*　*　*

Now it was perfectly all right, some "untouchables"

declared, for those political bodies to give in to this brash new journalism, but certainly the "big wheels" of the town were above that sort of treatment. Or were they?

The classic illustration of the newspaper's determination to publish all the news came within a few months of the first issue.

The showdown came at the worst of times. In the Depression, more and more banks were failing. One suburban bank was closed by state officials in 1932, and two of its officers were jailed. The community was bitter. Faith in banks was waning, and many a depositor withdrew his small savings and tucked them under a mattress.

At the depth of this depression, the news wire carried a story that a Kentuckian was suing one of Pottstown's four banks for almost a half-million dollars. Such a blow could have ugly repercussions. There could be a run on the bank, and a charge of causing such a run could be serious!

But the dedicated Mercury decided to risk all consequences. Hill himself handled the story. He telephoned the bank president for comment.

"We have a news association report here that Edward Ream, of Louisville, Kentucky, is suing your bank for $415,514," Hill told the bank president.

The reaction was quick.

"You can't print that," he snapped.

"Oh, yes we can, and will," Hill firmly replied. "We'd like to have your comment."

"Don't you dare print that!" was the parting shot from the bank.

Hill and Bill Hiester went out for a cup of coffee a few minutes later that morning. As they walked on the main street, an automobile drew abreast of them, and John L. Schulz, one of Pottstown's leading industrialists, a bank director and a leader in community life, called them.

"Will you two see Mr. Storb at his home?" he importuned.

John W. Storb, the bank president, was a state legislator, a

30

Republican leader and one of the richest men in Pottstown. He had vast real estate holdings in the business section. He was the type usually tagged as the man who "owns the town."

The two newspapermen walked to Storb's mansion, and were ushered into the drawing room. "Would you like a glass of wine?" Storb asked. The mere mention of wine in mid-morning was so repulsive it was easy to decline.

As the conference proceeded, the newspapermen insisted they planned to print all the news, all the time. Storb (at least 35 years their senior) said the man bringing the suit had no basis for the claim. He backed up this assertion by having his Philadelphia lawyer issue a similar statement. Then Storb took another tack—at least The Mercury could soften the story. It was agreed.

"With your permission to use the story, we'll tone it down," the two newsmen told Storb. Everybody seemed satisfied, and the story was published on Page One.

To fortify his claim of the bank's solvency, Storb placed a half-page advertisement in the paper. Lines did form at the bank on its next working day, but fortunately, only a few depositors withdrew their money.

Chapter 4

A GOOD BEGINNING

Within a year of its founding, The Mercury had an opportunity to perform a public service and endear itself to "the overburdened taxpayer." Taxes were high, the citizens complained, and made more burdensome because of lack of employment in the Depression years. The Mercury saw places where borough administrative costs might be cut, and it embarked on an all-out campaign to cut taxes.

A borough councilman of the minority party, quite vocal and publicity-conscious, was enlisted to suggest a tax decrease. The majority party demurred. But The Mercury thumped the tub with such élan that the council bent to the public will, and lopped off a mill of the tax. The school district followed suit with a three-mill slash.

That won public acclaim, but The Mercury took no bows. This set the policy for all future victories. The laurels went to the public-spirited councilman who led the fight in the tax issue. The kudos in future victories went to those who "fronted" for the campaigns.

The Mercury notched many a victory, and the Pottstown Chamber of Commerce, often censured editorially for lack of initiative, responded after many years with unstinting praise for the newspaper's leadership.

Victories came quite easily in the early years because there were so many conquests to make. Pottstown, in the throes of the Depression, needed many improvements.

This was the 20th century, but Pottstown still was dumping raw human sewage into its creek and river; and some open "runs" through the community were filth-strewn and malodorous. There was but a short inadequate sewer system. At least half the community's homes was not hooked up with it.

The schools were housed in dark, dingy firetraps. Toilet facilities were outdoors. Most had no electric lights.

Human waste was disposed of in pits beneath "backyard bungalows" that frequently had to be dredged. Septic tanks to disintegrate the waste were unpopular.

Pottstown was governed by an unwieldy body of 20 councilmen. The police department and its chief of police were appointed at the whim of the council. When council's political complexion changed, so did the police. The "ins" were "outs." There was no such thing as civil service; there were no examinations for police. In fact, one policeman was unable to read or write.

Streets were in deplorable condition. Pottstown's main street was brick-paved, and this, mind you, in the middle 1930's. There was no traffic control except one hand-controlled traffic semaphore at the town's busiest intersection. The signal was anchored in a sturdy concrete base. Many a drunk bashed his auto against this—and often wound up in the hospital.

Pottstown's water company was privately owned. The water not only tasted bad, but it was hard to get connections, because the private firm restricted its service area.

Pottstown was crying for reform, and the taxpayer was willing to pay for services when The Mercury showed the way. The big landlords pleaded, "Don't print those editorials about paving the streets. It would cost us too much money!" So The Mercury editorialized for more paved streets.

Sewer extension came. The filthy runs were enclosed. The state stepped in to end the flushing of human excrement into the Schuylkill River.

The schools were rebuilt, the old firetraps abandoned and replaced by new fireproof well-lighted schools.

The police were placed under civil service rules, with examinations required before appointments were made. A professional police chief was employed, after a nationwide search and long periods of interviews and examinations by an out-of-town firm.

Pottstown borough council was limited to seven members—from 20—and the seven were given nominal salaries. Pottstown became one of the first communities in the state to install parking meters. To keep traffic flowing, a highly efficient traffic control system was installed. Streets were paved, and a long list of dirt roads improved.

*　*　*　*　*

The Mercury also had time to comfort the afflicted. Its heart was shown in hundreds of ways.

During the Depression, The Mercury found a family living in a chicken house, another in an unheated backyard shed. One family couldn't find living quarters at all so they raised a tent on public ground and tried to subsist that way. The Mercury ended this squalor.

Over the loud protests of the chief executive of the community and many contractors, The Mercury waged a loud and successful fight for low-cost government housing.

Some school children were unable to pay for a half-pint of the milk their "wealthier" classmates bought at recesstime. For some there was no Christmas. The Mercury remedied these.

The Mercury asked its readers to supply funds for relief of the poor and the hungry. The response was generous, and families were given daily supplies of milk, the poor in school got as much milk as the rich, there were toys and clothing and Christmas baskets for the underprivileged.

A Christmas fund for a spastic girl raised so much money that Pottstown was able to send her to a specialist for training and later to a special school. Many a fund was raised for the bereaved, the stricken.

*　*　*　*　*

When the Vietnam war broke out, The Mercury asked its readers for funds to airmail the paper to all Pottstown servicemen in the fighting areas. Several hundred servicemen in Vietnam and Korea receive the paper daily through this "Bundles for Buddies" operation.

Editorially, The Mercury won many honors in its first 35 years.

Its voice was heard not only in its small community, but throughout the state and even the nation.

Its achievements were chronicled on the front pages of newspapers from the Atlantic to the Pacific. Its crusades were republished in large and small newspapers. Pennsylvania's legislature drew up a resolution to commend The Mercury for an exposé of inhuman conditions in state mental hospitals. Because of The Mercury's alertness, the Pentagon clamped down on cleverly-worded insurance solicitation which led parents to believe the company had connections with the U.S. Government.

Two universities cited The Mercury for community service after it had exposed the sad plight of the Pottstown Negro— long before the Supreme Court decisions against discrimination. The National Conference of Catholics and Jews applauded The Mercury for "brotherly love." Safety campaigns brought The Mercury many scrolls and trophies from state and nation. A national council of religious writers commended The Mercury for its church coverage.

The National Board of Fire Underwriters awarded The Mercury $500 and a gold medal for its crusade against fire hazards in the public schools. In competition with the largest papers of the state, The Mercury consistently won top honors in editorial excellence in Pennsylvania Society of Newspaper Editors competition. American Telephone and Telegraph Company, in conjunction with the American Newspaper Publishers Association, rated The Mercury in 1962 "the outstanding small newspaper in the United States."

In a few years, The Mercury had become a vital part of Pottstonians' lives. Oddly enough, some subscribers complained there was too much to read in it; they couldn't find time enough to digest all the news. As the newspaper's prestige grew, public opinion became unified and dependable. When the newspaper showed them the light, the readers acted.

BEST EDITORIAL STAFF in the early years of the Pottstown Mercury was this 1946-1948 group that won most state and national honors in 37 years. Standing, left to right, were Joseph Capaldi, John Binder, William M. Hiester, Frank J. Dostal, Shandy Hill, Mary Jane Fegley, Gordon Hemmerly, Charles Treleven, Harry Toland; kneeling, Gary L. Trollinger, Edward Rosenberg and Fred Selby.

Most beneficial was the restoration of pride to the community. Pottstown became proud of its progress; the citizens beamed when more favorable publicity came its way (mostly directed to other communications media by The Mercury). Twice, the community was nominated for "All-American City" awards. For four straight years, Washington gave it "cleanest city" plaques.

* * * * *

During all this activity, The Mercury became known widely as a "proving ground for young newspaperman." Newspaper executives often visited to survey the editorial operation, while some newspapers asked The Mercury to place interns on its staff. One summer, a contingent of seven journalism pupils of the Richmond, Va., Professional Institute descended on The Mercury "to help get out the paper."

"The Shandy Hill School of Journalism" was a hard, demanding classroom, yet the pupils appreciated the guidance and the opportunity for "gee whiz" chances to investigate, to develop a style. Those who survived the rigors of the "Shandy Hill School of Journalism" went far in the realm of metropolitan journalism.

J. Douglas Perry, dean of the school of journalism at Temple University, Philadelphia, introduced Hill at a Sigma Delta Chi dinner as "the man who hired and fired more reporters than anybody in the business."

This was a slight exaggeration. True, The Mercury attracted some misfits, just as all other businesses do. The editor often laughingly mused, "We get them all here, but we never let that deter us in our determination to teach them how to write." It was disappointing many times, and it was a wonder The Mercury was able to publish while a war of attrition continued—a war in which the large daily recruited from the small-town paper, able to lure the employee with a couple of dollars more in salary a week.

One nearby Pennsylvania newspaper combination at one

JOURNALISTIC FRIENDS were these Associated Press editors and general manager of the AP. The newspapermen were elected to AP association offices. Left to right: James Krider, Johnston; Hill; Harry Stacks, Lancaster; Wes Gallagher, AP general manager; C. Earl Miller, Greenville; and S. Parnell Lewis, Foster.

time had 15 former Mercury men on its two staffs.

The neophytes were taught that a newspaper has only one function—public service. The paper's selling commodity is news, and the news is to be guarded jealously.

That property right to news became almost an obsession with Hill. He smarted so much when his news was pirated that he took a radio station into court. The Pennsylvania Supreme Court ruled that there is indeed a property right in news, and "a radio broadcaster who, without license, permission or authority, uses local news items published in a local newspaper and gathered by the newspaper through special services and at considerable expense, thereby invades the newspaper owner's property right and is subject to liability for unfair competition."

It was the first time in Pennsylvania such a legal decision was made.

It is no easy task for an editor to keep his editorial staff from flagging in a newspaper monopoly town, as Pottstown was. It took gall for the whipcracker to demand production, including quality, diversity and interest. But the good newspaperman responded. The staff enjoyed doing a good job and being a major participant in a good product. The staffers glowed when men of their profession characterized The Mercury as one of the best small-town newspapers in the nation.

For a time, interest in their work might be heightened by competition. The newspaperman still beams over his "beats," although they are few and far between these days. But what happens when there is no newspaper competition?

Hill drove his writers hard with a Hearstian dictum: "Get the story first, but first get it right!" When a local radio station offered token competition in the late 1940's staffers were taught how to bottle up sources. It was not unusual for reporters to get promises from officials that they'd "hold" stories no matter when the news broke. The result was exclusive news—and the staffers got bigger bylines and bigger checks.

The Mercury was able to present news that couldn't be found or heard or seen elsewhere, news not in the metropolitan newspapers, news with its edge not taken off by prior broadcast or televising.

Chapter 5

BARK HEARD 'ROUND THE NATION

The low affectionate whine of the dog Jada, as he sniffed the package from his master, resounded in the halls of Congress, disturbed entrenched Pentagon officials, and echoed in every military and naval establishment of the United States.

The five-year-old thoroughbred collie became famous in his home community of Pottstown and quite infamous in insurance circles as far away as Dallas, Texas.

The whine, amplified by the loud voice of a small-town newspaper, caused a national stir. The Pottstown Mercury effectively enlisted congressmen and senators from two great states, as well as the Defense and Post Office Departments, to end "deceptive practices" by mail-order insurance companies and the frightening of mothers with sons in the service.

Soon after The Mercury's exposure of questionable insurance solicitation, other branches of the United States Government were looking for what the Federal Trade Commission said were "pitfalls . . . in mail-order insurance policies." The Federal Trade Commission's Bureau of Deceptive Practices investigated claims of false and misleading acts in direct-mail and newspaper advertising, and as late as December, 1967, issued "cease-and-desist" orders to firms that came within this purview.

The continued repercussion from its revelations indicated how a small newspaper's voice could be heard beyond its community's limits. It was an achievement that brought honors to the newspaper. How many heartbreaks it prevented never will be ascertained, but there must have been many.

Before this exposé The Mercury had harvested many local and state honors. This time its name resounded throughout the nation. But never before had it aligned on its side such famous personages as Senators Lyndon B. Johnson and Ralph W. Yarborough, of Texas, and Joseph S. Clark, of Pennsylvania; Federal Trade Commissioner Earl W. Kintner, Secretary of Defense Thomas S. Gates, Jr., Postmaster General Arthur Summerfield, and the top brass of the armed services establishment.

* * * * *

The wide-sweeping probe was begun by Shandy Hill to learn how mail-order insurance companies obtained the names and home addresses of servicemen and their families in order to make solicitations. It developed into a full-blown Washington inquiry into misleading and deceptive practices in connection with the sale of insurance in the mail-order field.

The investigation was begun by The Mercury when it learned that mothers were enticed by cleverly-worded sales promotion letters offering insurance on their sons in the service, "since the government no longer issues $10,000 life insurance to service personnel."

This was factual. The Government had ended that insurance benefit at the conclusion of the Korean conflict. Life insurance up to $10,000 was made available again by the Government to each member of the armed forces in September, 1965 (but this was five years after The Mercury probe).

The letters soliciting mail-order insurance were signed, for the most part, by retired Air Force or Army officers. Such signatures—and assurances that "I myself am retired from the service and both sympathize and envy your boy in the experience that awaits him in his exciting life ahead"—lent weight to the purchase pleas.

The letters led many parents to believe the United States Government was behind the deal. Some companies used windowed brown envelopes similar to those used by the United States in mailing out checks and other documents.

After The Mercury exposé, the Government issued a warning about such envelopes, which identified the sender by some designation such as "Veterans Insurance Division." The government warning practically paralleled what The Mercury had uncovered.

The Mercury cautioned care by recipients of the letters, and stressed the fact that Pennsylvania insurance commissioners found the mail-order insurance companies not registered in the state. "It would be hard to process claims in the courts because of the inability to obtain service upon companies that have no Pennsylvania addresses," Pennsylvania State Insurance Commissioner Francis R. Smith said.

Next, well-established Pennsylvania registered insurance companies said they could furnish life insurance at much less cost.

But the gnawing questions raised by The Mercury were:

—How did the lists of names of United States service personnel fall into the hands of insurance solicitors?

—Were the lists obtained by devious methods?

—Were the insurance companies authorized to do business on Army posts or in Pennsylvania?

—Who and what were the insurance companies?

The Mercury exposé began on a low and humorous note. It ended in a stunning silence of Army, Navy, and Air Force voices that might have been whispering lists of service personnel—perhaps for a price!

Senator Yarborough, after The Mercury completed its probe, said, "I recall that retired officers who were hired by the companies were supplying the names. They were obtaining the names, if my memory is correct, through contacts in the Defense Department.

* * * * *

Jada started it all. Innocently enough. The brown and white collie never knew what would result when his young master, Jack R. Sotter, Jr., addressed a package of soiled laundry and civilian clothes to his pet in Pottstown.

Jack had been summoned to Fort Knox, Kentucky, in

1960 to pay a six-month training obligation he owed the United States Army through the Pennsylvania National Guard. When issued GI clothes, Jack bundled his soiled linen and clothes and sent it by Railway Express to his mother. A fun-loving woman, Mrs. J. R. Sotter, Sr. shot back a note chiding him: "You dog! If you'd have washed the clothing it wouldn't have cost so much for expressage."

Jack never answered the note. He fired back another and heavier box of linen. As a joke this time he addressed it to his dog, Jada Sotter. This, too, he sent collect.

These incidents were treated as just a family joke even after Jack's mother received a letter from the Parents Counseling Service, Dallas, Texas, suggesting she buy life insurance on her son. Her husband was a Pottstown insurance broker, so she certainly had no need for insurance counseling. She tossed the sales letter into a waste basket without even mentioning the incident.

But when a similar letter came to the Sotter home, addressed to Mrs. Jada Sotter, the father's curiosity was aroused. Jacob R. Sotter saw in it a feature story, and brought it to Shandy Hill. The newspaper saw further implications.

Sotter, Sr., was struck by an attention-getter on the envelope: "This is an important message regarding your SON," the last word capitalized. The return address on the envelope read: "Colonel Morris Martin (USAF, Ret.), Dallas, Texas."

The Mercury story, complete with pictures of Jada, his master and the elder Sotters, brought a flood of mail from other parents of servicemen who had received this type of solicitation.

Mothers of two servicemen in Fort Jackson, S.C., had received insurance solicitation letters postmarked Fort Worth, Texas. Other mail came from Wichita Falls, Texas, Phoenix, Ariz., and Elba, Ala. Most were signed by retired Air Force officers, but the Alabama letter came in the name of a Navy man from San Diego, Calif.

44

Some service centers may have gotten wind of the solicitation. For two parents received letters from the Air Force Lackland Military Training Center, in Texas, warning: "You may receive solicitations for various items. Some may infer sponsorship by the Air Force. But the Air Force neither encourages nor discourages the purchase of any product, service or insurance."

The Federal Trade Commission, years later, similarly warned: "If your son has recently entered the Armed Forces of the United States your morning mail may contain an envelope bearing the name of a designated insurance company and containing such wording as 'Special Armed Forces Policy Enclosed.'

"Upon opening the envelope you will find a form letter and what appears to be a complete life insurance policy. The form letter will state that since your son has entered the Armed Forces and met the physical requirements he is eligible for a 'Special Low-Cost $10,000 Military Life Insurance Company.' . . . You may believe, as many parents have, that the insurance thus offered is being made available to you by the United States Government. In fact, life insurance has been made available by the government to each member of the Armed Forces since September, 1965 . . . ."

The Mercury asked Senator Joseph S. Clark and U. S. Representative John A. LaFore, Jr., in whose constituency Pottstown was located, to probe the letters. Clark asked the Defense Department to "identify the parties responsible for the release of names." Ex-servicemen's groups, the American Legion and the Veterans of Foreign Wars directed their national organizations to look into the matter.

Hill telephoned Fort Knox where Lt. Col. Walter K. Freeland, public information officer, said his superiors would begin an investigation. He said he had no way of knowing how the servicemen's names were obtained.

The Mercury asked the Railway Express Company whether it knew how names were secured. A public relations man in its New York offices said the names did not come from the company.

Clark also asked Secretary of Defense Thomas S. Gates, Jr., to "look into the unfortunate use of the mails." He asked his personal and political friend, Senate Majority Leader Lyndon B. Johnson, of Texas, to make an investigation. The Mercury published future President Johnson's picture on Page One, probably the first time it was printed in Pottstown.

The Mercury made a ten-strike when it enlisted the aid of the Dallas, Texas, Times-Herald and offered the story exclusively on an exchange basis. Surely, the Times-Herald could do better investigative reporting personally and on the scene than The Mercury could do by telephone. So Bob Hollingsworth, Times-Herald managing editor, went to the Life Building, where the Parents Counseling Services letterhead said it had suites 1019-20. Hollingsworth found those offices vacant, but a maintenance man said he expected tenants to move in soon.

A background check showed Col. Morris Martin had retired in 1950 after 31 years in the Air Force. He was 58. He couldn't be reached for comment.

In fact, Hollingsworth reported, the retired military officers who signed the insurance-soliciting letters "were not anxious to say how they got the names." Armed services officials in the Pentagon said it was against regulations to divulge names of personnel in the services.

*   *   *   *   *

How news gets around! By this time, the full import of the probe was becoming known. Joe Killough, president of Sovereign Life, addressed a letter to The Mercury explaining how the servicemen's names could be obtained. He said the Reuben H. Donnelly (telephone books) and R. L. Polk (city directories) Companies make such lists available. He also commented that servicemen's names might be obtained from news accounts.

This, strangely enough, was paralleled by a Federal Trade

Commission booklet, "Pitfalls to Watch for in Mail Order Insurance Policies." This declared that such mail was addressed by a "private, commercial company which has obtained the names and addresses through hometown newspapers and other unofficial sources."

The "unofficial sources" angle was not amplified.

The Dallas Times-Herald sicked its Washington bureau onto the case. Democratic Senator Yarborough threw his weight behind the probe, and was quoted as saying he had heard "rumors" for years of "unfair" preferential treatment received "by some companies over the great bulk of the insurance industry," but he had "no definite, documented proof that insurers are furnished the information."

An unidentified Pentagon spokesman admitted, the Times-Herald said, that someone might be selling the lists. The Defense Department said years ago that someone at Fort Chaffee was selling lists. "Action" had been taken against him, the department said.

By this time, the chase was on. The National Association of Life Underwriters, through its Washington offices, also asked for an investigation by the Defense Department. Senator Clark demanded that Earl W. Kintner, chairman of the Federal Trade Commission, delve into the situation, "because the states can't regulate the improper acquisition of Federal Government mailing lists by out-of-state companies." Postmaster General Summerfield was asked to bar from use of the mails any company with "deceptive practices."

Officials worked quietly along the Potomac, but the word went out to military and naval installations that security regulations were to be tightened, and there was to be no more "procuring, or attempting to procure, or supplying roster listings of personnel for solicitation purposes," nor "the offering of unfair, improper and deceptive inducements to purchase or deal."

But not until seven years after The Mercury's exposé did the Federal Trade Commission issue a news release (on

November 23, 1967) announcing it had "substantially completed an investigation of alleged misleading and deceptive practices in the mail-order insurance industry."

The news release said, "The investigation covered the practices of approximately 72 companies, including nearly all of the important companies in the industry. . . By far the majority of these companies operate in a proper and forthright manner.

"This industry consists," the release continued, "of companies which sell insurance through advertising and other printed promotional matter sent by mail to residents of various states. Many of the companies are not subject to effective state regulation as they are not licensed in the state to which the mailings are sent . . . . The states, therefore, are unable to enforce effectively any regulation they might impose. These companies are subject to Federal Trade Commission regulation."

Then the Commission listed eight "primary practices used which appear to be misleading and deceptive."

Number One on the list was the practice inveighed against by The Mercury: "offering life insurance policies to the parents of servicemen with the implication that the insurance is being made available by the United States Government."

The wheels of government grind slowly, but exceedingly fine.

It was victory for The Mercury, and a great compliment was paid to Shandy Hill by Brig. Gen. William W. Berg, deputy assistant secretary of defense.

"In regards to the Jada Sotter incident of 1960," he wrote, "this incident was considered in the development of our present policy which prohibits the procuring, or attempting to procure, or supplying roster listings of Department of Defense personnel for solicitations purposes.

"To the credit of the internal monitoring policies of the military departments and to the life insurance industry, the practices of 1960 on indiscriminate roster procurement and utilization are no longer a problem. The absence of complaints or queries on this issue most forcefully bespeak the certainty of the department in this matter.

"Your interest in the welfare of our service personnel is appreciated."

Chapter 6

MR. JAMES P. CROW, ESQ.

Many thought Pottstown was too small a town to have a Negro "problem."

Most of Pottstown's 3,000 Negroes were tightly segregated into one small hilly section of the borough, derogatorily referred to as "Chicken Hill." Except to work, few Negroes left that restricted area to mingle with whites.

It was true these Negroes "knew their place." They didn't aspire to much more than menial jobs which just about provided livelihoods. They didn't make much trouble for the police. The crime rate was low.

But that didn't mean segregation did not flourish in this small clannish town. It did, despite the self-praise claim by the bigots that "we go to school together and have no trouble."

That was true, too, because the "Negro problem" didn't exist to a noticeable extent in the early 1940's. But discrimination was ever present.

This came to Shandy Hill's attention when a Pottstown labor leader pointed out that Negroes were not permitted to bowl in Pottstown's only public alley. He asked whether Hill would help "desegregate" the bowling alley.

There was no violent reaction, nothing like the explosions of 1967-68 in the South when Negroes concentrated on "opening" bowling alleys to their use. There was no racial violence such as erupted in Orangeburg, S.C., in 1968, when three Negro youths attempting to "liberate" a bowling alley were shot to death by police.

A few conferences and a bit of arguing with the proprietor convinced him that Negroes should be permitted to bowl there.

Intolerance for the Negro in the Pottstown area surfaced more openly when the Allegheny Conference of the Seventh-day Adventist church, a Negro body, announced plans to found a four-year junior college just outside Pottstown.

A site for the college was found, and the Seventh-day Adventists quietly went to work to acquire it. When word of the sale leaked out, the owner of the land, a retired physician, was the target of criticism from nearby farm owners, "prominent" officials and run-of-the-mill citizens. Loud was the insistence that the sale be abrogated.

There was sullen resentment even beyond the area. Town and rural residents declared no Negroes could invade "their" territory. This was understandable because the Negro effectively, albeit quietly, had been segregated.

Just a few miles from the proposed Negro college site was a large municipality of 4,000 which boasted that no Negro had ever lived within its borders and never would! There were reports of secret agreements that no home owner ever would sell to a Negro, no real estate dealer would rent or sell living space to a black man. Naturally, these reports never could be run down. But even today, no Negro lives in that community.

A strident Mercury editorial campaign, in line with the newspaper's duty to fight for the community, to give voice to the weak, shattered the barriers of bigotry and paved the way for the Seventh-day Adventists to realize their goal. The editorial campaign was long; the area was sullen, but tolerance won out.

On the 575-acre site in beautiful rolling, verdant farm country, the church body erected buildings that teach and house almost 400 students annually. No longer was vocal opposition registered. No longer were private protest meetings held.

Recalling this early struggle, W. A. Thompson, president of Allegheny East Conference of the Seventh-day Adventist church, which included Pennsylvania, New Jersey, Delaware, Maryland and Virginia, said:

51

"As we reminisce concerning the beginning of our Christian educational program in this area, we fondly remember the way that you, through The Mercury, defended our entrance into this section. We needed a friend in a desperate way and you came forward to help us.

"You had your reading public to know that they should not judge a group before giving them a chance to prove themselves. This has marked your attitude of fairness through the years. Your editorials rang true. The reading public saw that The Mercury had taken its stand. We attempted to do our best to uphold the confidence that you showed to us, and as a result the fear and near hysteria subsided.

"Never once have we forgotten The Mercury and your strong editorial force. Present and future successes of the Allegheny East Conference and the Pine Forge Academy are firmly based on the good beginning that you assisted them to have. May God ever bless and keep you as a champion of the underdog."

Many of the Academy students later went on to colleges to become prominent in the sciences, medicine, law, ministry and teaching.

The Mercury's crusading did not go unnoticed by the Allegheny officials quietly continuing their quest for higher educational facilities. In many newspaper campaigns there is no recognition when a battle is won. Not so in this case. From many churchmen came praise.

Wrote Harold D. Singleton, secretary of the North American Regional department of the general conference of Seventh-day Adventists:

"You were our champion when thumbs were turned down against us and our plans to establish an academy at Pine Forge.

"Non-whites had never lived independent lives in the Manatawny Valley (where the school was situated) so we were setting a precedent.

"Even though you did not know us, you were drawn to

our side by your vigorous conception of right prevailing. We are glad the years intervening justified your confidence and unflagging support."

Likewise, Ralph S. Watts, Sr., vice president of the Seventh-day Adventist General Conference, said, "The Seventh-day Adventists will always feel a sense of deep gratitude to you for the forthright and unequivocal manner in which you came to grips with false rumors and took your stand editorially in The Mercury at the side of right. The years proved the Adventists have made the contribution to better civic and spiritual life you declared they would."

Robert H. Pierson, president of the general conference of the Seventh-day Adventists, praised the battle against prejudice. He said:

"You played an important part in the growth and development of our work. Then we were without friends, unknown, and considered an undesirable irritant in the area. We appreciate the role you played in allaying prejudice, placating fears and clearing the air of disenchanted ideas and imaginary objections."

*   *   *   *   *

The Mercury pondered this small victory when the Supreme Court handed down its public school desegregation decision on May 17, 1954. Had we educated our people to respect the human rights of the black man?

The Supreme Court decision made it clear that the 14th Amendment was deemed to preclude segregation in the public schools. Pottstown wasn't concerned with this. Its schools were desegregated. But would the decision have any bearing on segregation of other kinds? The court already had indicated in a number of ways that there would be repercussions in other fields. It vacated and remanded, "for consideration in the light of the segregation cases," lower court decisions permitting segregation in public parks, a Louisiana and a Florida university, and a California housing project.

What was the status of the Pottstown Negro? Some said Pottstown was a good town for Negroes. There was no persecution here, if that was to count as a score for the white side.

A Negro leader said, "It's not a bad town at all. But we are treated as Negroes." That meant the Negro was tolerated on some levels but not accepted in fact as an equal.

This was easy to ascertain. What The Mercury could not learn was whether Pottstown was ready for the shock of learning exactly how it was setting apart the Negro from the life of the community. It would be a brutal shock, especially for a small town where admittance to the brotherhood of man is slow, where you can't make people love each other by passing a law.

The Mercury embarked on an in-depth investigation of the Negro's lot in the community, just a month after the Supreme Court decision. It shocked the "tolerant" whites all right, arousing fire in all walks of life. It aroused other communities, too. The Mercury's seven-part series was reprinted widely, especially in two Negro weeklies, the Pittsburgh Courier and the Baltimore Afro-American. But two "white" daily newspapers below the Mason-Dixon Line used the articles, too. They were reprinted by Henry Belk in the Goldsboro, N.C., News-Argus, and by Talbot Patrick in the Rock Hill, S.C., Herald. The series drew much editorial attention in Southern papers.

* * * * *

The look at Mr. James P. Crow, Esq., in Pottstown should have caused some red faces even among the "tolerant" whites, because it showed:

—Not a single Negro was a member of a service club. Kiwanis, Rotary, the Optimists, American Business Club, Lions, all shunned him.

—Not a Negro was a member of a fraternity or social club. This included the Eagles, Moose, Orioles, Odd Fellows, Knights of Columbus, Elks, Owls and others. Some said they wouldn't admit a Negro; others said none ever applied.

—No Negro was a member of a "white" veterans organization, such as the American Legion, Veterans of Foreign Wars or Amvets.

—The local country club, Brookside, had no Negro member.

—No Negro worked in other than a janitorial capacity for any of the three local public utilities, Philadelphia Electric Company, Pottstown Rapid Transit Company or Bell Telephone Company of Pennsylvania.

—Not one Negro, male or female, was a salesman or salesgirl in a Pottstown store.

—Only one Negro, a woman, had an "office job" in Pottstown.

—No Negro girl ever had been admitted to the Pottstown Hospital School for Nurses.

—Only one Negro ever worked as a nurse in the two Pottstown hospitals.

—No Negro ever had been a mail carrier for the Pottstown Post Office.

—No Negro ever had worked for the Pottstown public school system, except as a janitor.

—No Negro was a member of Pottstown's three volunteer fire companies.

—Fewer than 200 Negroes worked in local industry, and not one in the textile industry.

—A Negro could not be buried in a Pottstown cemetery. His body had to be taken out of town.

Small wonder, then, that the Charleston, S.C., News-Courier asked, "Is the Negro worse off, is there more discrimination against him, in the South or in an average Northern community, such as Pottstown, Pennsylvania?"

The newspaper answered the question with the assertion, "In Charleston there are Negro nurses, mailmen, firemen, policemen, salesgirls, stenographers, teachers, doctors."

*   *   *   *   *

The editor knew the pestilence of intolerance could not be

eradicated by the Supreme Court's legal decision, at least not overnight.

But some barriers to progress were removed. In a talk to a conference of the Allegheny conference of the Seventh-day Adventists in July, 1956, Shandy Hill said:

"A few years ago, the superintendent of public schools recoiled in horror when we told him our crusade for anti-discrimination would be helped considerably if the school board were to hire a Negro teacher. We got nowhere until this year, however, and the first Negro woman teacher in Pottstown's history will begin to teach in September.

"Just a short few days ago, the Bell Telephone Company in Pottstown proudly announced it was employing its first Negro."

Hill continued, "We do not look on this as personal victories," but he added prophetically, "The time is coming quickly when color will be no barrier to any jobs—good jobs—and equal pay."

*   *   *   *   *

The acceptance of this Mr. James P. Crow, Esq., series outside of Pottstown was remarkable.

The Mercury received a salute from the curators of Lincoln University in Jefferson, Mo., "in recognition of a model, vigorous, and resourceful newspaper whose enlightening exposure of subtle race discriminatory practices stems from a publishing enterprise of high motive." The salute commended The Mercury for helping to make Pottstown "a model of neighborly love and justice."

The Mercury also received from the National Conference of Christians and Jews a brotherhood award for "outstanding contributions promoting the cause of goodwill and understanding, thereby fostering amity, justice and cooperation among all people helping to eliminate the intergroup prejudices which disfigure and distort religious, business, social and political relations."

The Pennsylvania Society of Newspaper Editors found the series worthy of an editorial excellence award.

Chapter 7

HAS THE NEGRO MADE PROGRESS?

Admittance to the brotherhood of man is slow indeed. The Pottstown Negro had no place to buy a drink except in the black St. James Hotel, until the state government in 1954 ended this discrimination, and today he's admitted to all public drinking and eating places. Now the Negro has white-collar jobs, the Negro woman is a nurse, a stenographer, a teacher.

But it took many years, so many in fact, that The Mercury had to try to hurry the Negro's admittance to the brotherhood of man by making another survey in 1964. It showed progress still was impeded.

The story of this recapitulation is told by The Philadelphia Bulletin's Paul Levy, a Mercury "graduate." Here it goes:

"The note was rolled into the typewriter when I walked in.

" 'It's been ten years since *The Mercury* checked to see if the Negro in Pottstown is making any progress,' the note began.

"It went on to explain that in 1954, shortly after the U. S. Supreme Court handed down its famed school desegregation ruling to begin a new era in civil rights in America, another Mercury reporter had been assigned to look into the situation.

"The reporter found the Negro in Pottstown at the very lowest rung of the borough's economic and social ladder.

" 'Has he climbed any steps since then?' the note concluded, 'It's time to find out.'

"The note was signed—Shandy Hill.

"For weeks I checked.

"Good housing and apartments were still closed to Negroes.

"White-collar jobs were still for white faces.

"Management positions, in business, in industry, even in borough hall, still carried a 'white only' sign.

"Even fighting fires was still an all white, all volunteer job, even though supported by borough taxes.

"I took the facts and the conclusions to Shandy Hill, and laid them out.

" 'It's going to embarrass a lot of advertisers and the town even more,' I explained.

" 'If it's true, write it,' he replied, 'and we'll print it.'

"It was written—ten articles, more than 10,000 words.

"As each article was written and printed, the town seethed a little more, and by the time the fifth or sixth one arrived on the doorsteps, the communications had become a two-way street.

"The letters started pouring in—to Hill, to the Letters to the Editor column, and to me.

"Mine started off almost identically, as if they had been punched out on a mindless xerox machine:

" 'Dear Nigger Lover:'

"I thought the letters were funny.

"Shandy Hill took them as a compliment.

" 'You've pricked the conscience of the town,' he explained, 'and said what had to be said.'

"Then, almost in an afterthought that could have served as his creed for all the years he served as The Mercury's guardian hand, he added:

" 'A newspaper has to serve as the conscience of its town.'

"The Mercury did this—and so did Hill.

"Not every story—like the one on the Negro in Potts-town—was intended to sear the town's collective conscience.

"I wrote scores of articles that helped in passing the $6-million bond issue that gave Pottstown clean water.

"I wrote even more articles that gave the borough the push it needed to acquire the old post office for a modern library befitting Pottstown.

"Other reporters did the same—pushing for modern

mercury vapor lighting, downtown 'park-and-shop lots,' improved schools, school mergers to overcome petty inter-township jealousies in the name of better education.

"These were the crusades that gave The Mercury a national name in journalism, a name that meant good, honest, harddriving news gathering.

"But there was more than this, more than just crusades.

"There was detailed coverage of the borough and township governments, the kind that allows the public to know and participate in the decision-making process before the decision, out-of-the-blue, suddenly became law one day.

"There was the same detailed coverage of the town and its people, their trips, their sports, their social activities, their likes and dislikes and desires and aspirations.

"When there was a half-inch left at the bottom of a column of type, it wasn't filled by a note on the height of the Washington Monument or the length of the Mississippi River, as is done in all too many papers.

"It was filled with a short note that Johnny Jones fell out of a tree and broke his arm. It was more interesting because Johnny Jones might have been your neighbor, and you may not have known about it.

"I cover the White House now.

"I have a fancy title, Washington correspondent, but the job is the same—letting the people (this time those who read The Philadelphia Bulletin) know what their government is doing. [Editor's note: Levy was sent to cover the Vietnam war in 1968.]

"If there were more papers like The Mercury in the country, the people would know more about their government—why the budget is over $100 billion, how we went from 15,000 to 466,000 in Vietnam, what is really being done to fight crime in the streets.

"When President Johnson goes to his ranch in Texas, I and the rest of the White House press tag along.

"The press stays in San Antonio and the local paper is The San Antonio Light.

"It has a wonderful motto that I always feel The Mercury and Shandy Hill—for he is, in a very real sense, The Mercury—should adopt.

" 'Give Light, and the People Shall Find Their Own Way.'

"For thirty years, Shandy Hill has given that light."

Chapter 8

ALL EQUAL HERE

The "sensitive" use of the word Negro, which so many editors pondered (and still find difficult) gave The Mercury no trouble.

The Mercury just didn't use the word "Negro" to identify one who committed a crime, unless it was necessary. The Mercury never said Joe Magyar, a Hungarian, was arrested for drunken driving, or that Staislauf Quicklinski, a Pole, raped a Chinese, or Elmer Panofsky, a Ukrainian, robbed a house. So why use "Negro"?

When The Mercury eliminated this reference (and never used the word "colored" because the editors just couldn't comprehend what that generalization included), a smattering of praise came from the black element of the community, and the sky didn't fall down on the white community. There was no comment, except a jab by a slightly stoned woman who called the editor a "nigger lover" at a country club dinner.

Long before the state passed its human relations commission and job anti-discrimination law, The Mercury crusaded for equal opportunities for Negroes. The newspaper formed a human relations committee of prominent local citizens to investigate the Negro's place in the community. Shandy Hill prevailed upon Pottstown School Board to hire its first Negro teacher, but not until after a superintendent of schools brushed off original attempts with an order: "Send your Negro teachers to Coatesville. They have segregated schools there." (Coatesville, 20 miles south of Pottstown, indeed had a totally segregated school until the state ordered it desegregated in 1968). That superintendent of schools resigned in a short time, and his successor placed Negro teachers in the schools.

The Mercury got the first Negro employee into the Firestone Tire and Rubber Company, and convinced local bowling alleys to stop barring blacks on bowling teams.

The Mercury's news columns were "desegregated" for years before the nationwide agitation erupted. Negro achievers of honors worthy of illustration saw their pictures in the newspaper, and not next to the classified pages, either.

The Mercury used pictures and stories of Negro brides on the social pages. There have been no audible squawks, no subscription cancellations.

How many editors today have gone the whole route and eliminated racial distinctions from their pages? Shandy Hill, at an Associated Press managing editors' conference, said, "Many editors thunder loftily in behalf of downtrodden minorities, but fail to examine the beam in their own eyes while calling attention to the moat elsewhere."

* * * * *

As the voices of the minorities were heard more loudly, as violence in the cities erupted in the 1960's, as the "poor people" marched in nonviolence in Washington, it was recalled that The Mercury even alerted its readers to another area of minority neglect when it had its own correspondent write of the poor Indian.

Kay O'Donnell, a Pottstown girl who was to become a Mercury internee, went to Wahpeton, North Dakota, in the summer of 1962 and did a series of seven articles from a boarding school for Indians there. The Mercury asked: "Are these wards of the United States discriminated against?" and Miss O'Donnell answered.

She spent a summer with orphaned or abandoned Sioux and Chippewa children, mostly from the Sisseton reservation, south of Wahpeton. Most of the children were emotionally or mentally retarded. She told readers, "Some of the little ones do not know they are Indians. But the older children must learn they are different and supposedly second-class

63

citizens." Some regarded the school as a prison. Teachers said the highest insult was to call another a "white man."

This series was done before America seriously pondered America's inhumanity to man. But it wasn't too early, even though Pottstown learned well ahead of some parts of the nation.

Chapter 9

A CITY MADE OVER

There was ample opportunity in Pottstown to make The Mercury into something more than a paper just published daily, something more than a mirror of events. The community, frayed at the heels because of years of neglect, needed leadership. It called for making the newspaper into an institution of public service.

Admittedly, The Mercury's voice often was shrill, but experience over the years showed that the subscriber expected the newspaper to take a stand, not straddle important issues. Even though many readers disagreed many times, they still understood that The Mercury's position resulted from a conviction that its campaigns were in the public interest.

The reader was educated to become a part of government, an institution he had neglected for years. The process was slow, but passage of the years indicated he wanted good men and women to represent him. He didn't want to be pushed around by politicians.

The Mercury learned, too, that the reader wanted to know why some misguided officials withheld news, or transacted the public business behind closed doors or in star-chamber sessions. The newspaper told why, and the reader sought more news about the obstacles thrown into reporters' paths.

When the newspaper harped on these secret sessions, some held in private homes, the public reacted and "threw out the rascals" at the polling places. The Mercury broke down the barriers to public news sources long before the Pennsylvania Legislature passed a law in the 1960's, forbidding elected bodies to transact public business behind closed doors.

All the while, it kept the black smoke rolling out of the factory chimneys. When Pottstown prospered, The Mercury prospered.

It is not immodest to say that under Shandy Hill's direction, The Mercury remade Pottstown. It remade it physically—not under urban redevelopment sponsorship, which was to come a decade later; not under federal aid, which was sparse in those redevelopment years; it was homemade—this remaking.

The Mercury remade Pottstown's laws. It changed its government from a hodgepodge into a progressive, efficient, vital administrative force. It changed its thinking, for the newspaper created an informed public opinion that couldn't help but alter the way of government. The Mercury aroused the community from a lethargy and showed it the way in every field of man's endeavor. Because of ingrained problems, it took years to overcome. But come it did.

In its dedication to the public welfare, The Mercury earned prestige. Citizens beat a path to its door to ask whether they could help. The Mercury had the confidence of the public. It became a vital part of Pottstonians' lives. They didn't seem able to live without it. Public opinion became unified, dependable.

Certainly, The Mercury was taken to task by readers with self-interest or opposing viewpoints, but few would deny that the newspaper did stand by its principles—it was a newspaper working in the public interest.

The Mercury treated friend and foe alike. It was not deterred by fear of reprisals.

The newspaper said it would expose incompetence and fraud in government. It would not allow bigotry or prejudice to dull its blows for brotherly love, for equal opportunity to all. There were no castes in The Mercury's columns—the citizen on the other side of the railroad track was accorded the same treatment as the millionaire in his marble halls.

*   *   *   *   *

One word might describe Pottstown's 1931 physical appearance: primitive. The thoughtful editor, therefore, could not help but see that much reform was needed; not reform because it was an evil community (it wasn't), but reform because the taxpayer was entitled to some of the better things of life.

Pottstown just grew. It was settled shortly after 1700 when John Penn was granted large tracts of land by his father, William Penn. It prospered when it became the center of the iron and steel industry before the Revolutionary War. One of the early ironmongers was John Potts, who bought 990 acres in 1752, laid out a town on this tract and named it for himself. The town was incorporated as a borough in 1815.

By this time, it was a flourishing village, the center of a prosperous iron industry and the home of the Hill School, a boys' preparatory school, which was to become nationally known.

The iron industry flourished during the 1800's, but at the turn of the twentieth century, most of the privately owned firms were taken over by great corporations. Instead of nail works and small structural steel plants, the town found its large industry in the hands of the Bethlehem Steel Corporation, the Spicer Manufacturing Company and Doehler Die Casting Company. Textile mills sprang up in the early 1930's to give employment to women, but these faded from the scene when cheaper labor was found in the South.

Industrial employment was at a low ebb during the Depression. Apathy had settled over the town. Franklin D. Roosevelt, in a campaign speech, said, "Grass was growing in the middle of the streets." The Mercury "localized" this remark by setting up a picture of a large farm mower cutting the grass at Pottstown's busiest intersection.

Pottstown was so isolated in those Depression years that a local organization, in 1931, advocated keeping chain stores out of the community. An advertisement in The Mercury, dated October 28, 1931, and signed by the Pottstown Investment Company, Harold Weber, secretary, asked:

"Why are we losing industry?

67

"Why do we not secure new industry?

"Why are you out of work?

"How much is the chain store taking out of town?"

The answers were to be given at a public meeting, the advertisement promised, but if they were, they never were revealed.

* * * * *

Pottstown, too, was dull. It had a population of 19,430 in 1931, but it lacked the will to move forward. When The Mercury editorialized for civic improvements, the local government pleaded that it didn't want its somnolence disturbed. "Let a sleeping dog lie," it said.

The town's most prosperous landowner and banker made almost weekly visits to The Mercury to ask Hill, "Don't write those editorials about paving the streets. It costs too much money."

When the banker left the office, another crusading editorial was fashioned. But the complainer never relinquished his friendship with the editor.

Well should such editorials have been written. Less than a sixth of Pottstown's streets were paved in 1931. By 1967, after constant editorial prodding and after many features and news stories, Pottstown had improved practically every mile. It also had a modern vehicle bypass—backed by The Mercury—that took heavy truck traffic from its main thoroughfares.

Yet the street system was not as woeful as its sewer system. Sadly neglected, it posed a health problem. Its offshoots were eyesores. It may be difficult to believe, but as late as 1931, Pottstown was dumping its sewage (and this included raw human sewage) into creeks through the borough. What's more, some enterprising citizens were charging householders annual fees to be hooked up to this "private sewer system."

What sewage did not flow untreated into the Schuylkill

River was carried through 20 miles of pipe in the town to a "primary" sewage treatment plant. This plant allowed for little more than settling of solids, and minor treatment. Then the sewage was dumped into the river, to pollute the water that eventually flowed into Philadelphia.

Outhouses—the little backyard bungalows—were everywhere in town, endangering the public health.

But by 1967, less than five miles of city streets were without sewers. No outside toilets were in use. Houses unconnected to the sewer system had septic tanks. And the sewage plant—expanded so greatly that it served nearby communities—was approved by the state in compliance with the law that prohibited the pouring of untreated water into the river.

The unsightly smelly "runs" that coursed through the town, carrying fecal matter with other waste, were arched or covered. The last of these creeks was eliminated in 1965, when Bethlehem Steel expanded its plant.

All this was accomplished by the newspaper's frequent exposure of the dangers to health and limb. One of the most startling feature stories was written by a staffer assigned to become a sewer rat, to traverse the arched runs and to tell what he found.

*   *   *   *   *

All these improvements were bound to come, possibly even without newspaper support. The citizenry wouldn't continue to stand for this primitiveness. But The Mercury hastened the day.

Most laxity was in the field of government. The biggest achievement of The Mercury was to revamp the entire municipal structure to gain a more pliable governing body and to give each citizen better representation.

When The Mercury was founded, Pottstown had ten wards, each represented by two councilmen. This made for an inefficient body of 20, most prone to perform favors for

69

their friends. The loudest or the most vocal got improvements, what few they were, for their wards.

This government worked backwards, unbelievable as it may sound. The group got together, decided how much revenue was needed to turn the wheels of government the coming year and set the tax rate. Then the ruling power— be it Democratic or Republican—doled out the money to various departments, to police, streets, sewer, etc. There was no budget! State law did not require filing of such budgets until later.

In 1931, less than $200,000 was collected in taxes and expended by the borough. That meant $10.50 per citizen.

By 1967, Pottstown was a million-dollar corporation. Its 1967 budget was for $951,752 or almost $37.50 per person.

Naturally, borough services are more costly. The town has more police protection, more fire protection, better streets, municipal collection of garbage and other services, solidly advocated by The Mercury.

To the student of government, the most important thing that happened to Pottstown was the employment of a borough manager, a professional to take over the million-dollar corporation. He was responsible to council, but he practically had total sway; his ethics precluded political interference.

Up to this time, the borough government functioned—if it could be called that—with a number of autonomous departments, such as police, water, sewer and streets. All ostensibly were tied into a secretary's office, but the real direction came from an army of councilmen who ordered supervisors what to do and what not to do. Underlings obeyed, because their positions were at the whim of the politicians. They could be turned out of borough hall every time the political wind shifted—and frequently were. That there was no chaos in government never could be explained. The town existed, but it didn't flourish.

The Mercury wrote its first editorial urging a borough

manager on October 1, 1931, in its third issue! The Mercury wrote and wrote and wrote. Every Monday for years, the lead editorial plugged for the progressive move. For years and years, it appeared The Mercury was butting its head against a stone wall.

But finally, borough council adopted the manager form of government, and in March, 1945, almost 14 years later, the borough had its first nonpolitical administrator, Dow I. Sears. The appointment was a triumph of tenacity. Pottstown has had four borough managers from 1945 to 1968. One died. A second moved to a better paying job in New Jersey. The third went into private industry.

While The Mercury frequently failed to see eye to eye with Pottstown Chamber of Commerce (it often accused the Chamber of lacking in imagination as well as backbone), one of its present-day presidents, lawyer C. Edmund Wells, wrote to the membership in March, 1967: "A cornerstone in Pottstown's fortunate pattern of good government was laid years ago by the decision to initiate the borough manager system. In fact, Pottstown was one of the first major boroughs in the state to adopt the professional approach to local government administration. . . . The proposal (was) strongly supported by The Pottstown Mercury."

Pottstown, a pioneer in this movement, has been studied many times by many other municipalities.

*   *   *   *   *

Pottstown's cumbersome council of 20 members first was reduced to ten after strong editorial suggestion. Finally, came "the most outstanding governmental reform in fifty years," as Wells put it. It was ward reapportionment and reduction of council to seven men, one from each of seven new wards.

For many years, The Mercury had promoted this idea— long before the "one man, one vote" principle gained popularity in Washington and finally was enacted into law for the state. Pottstown had the same inequitabilities as the nation.

71

One ward had fewer than 100 registered voters; others had as many as 1,500.

The Mercury took its plan to civic club after civic club, trying to get a sponsor to take the case into court, where reapportionment had to be approved. Finally, in the early 1960's the Chamber of Commerce was induced to seek the reform, and Wells wrote: "Long advocated by The Pottstown Mercury . . . this cause lacked a sponsor until the Chamber . . . provided the pad for launching the move and financed, sponsored and supervised the project to complete achievement. Improvement in our common lot can be fairly attributed to efforts of dedicated persons."

*   *   *   *   *

Other progressive achievements were suggested by The Mercury, which thumped the tub with increasing vigor as time moved on.

After a Mercury editorial campaign, an airport was opened in 1948 during a time when every community believed it had to be on an airline route. Pottstown never got on a commercial airline route. But it had its airport.

The continuing flow of traffic was a problem, as automobile ownership increased and the streets became crowded. (mostly with double parkers who had to be pushed aside by a special policeman).

Merchants complained because the business section was cluttered with all-day parkers (although it frequently developed that the merchants themselves and their clerks were the culprits). The Mercury learned this when it made an exhaustive downtown survey, publishing lists of auto licenses occupying the same spaces for long periods of time.

Shandy Hill first proposed parking meters on Pottstown streets, not as a revenue gainer, but to keep traffic moving by permitting one-hour parking only. Borough council took up the plan, and in 1941 installed 350 meters (to the usual and baseless complaints that someone in borough hall got a 'rakeoff' when the contract was awarded). Since then hundreds more meters have been placed.

Meter installation did not relieve congestion on the streets. So The Mercury campaigned for off-street parking. The first lot was constructed in 1949. In 1967, there were nine lots, and merchants clamor for still more.

How did all this, and more, come about? Only by widening the horizons of men's thinking, only by becoming the leader in the community. The town had something to be proud about—its newspaper—and The Mercury never failed to front for the man on the street!

*   *   *   *   *

Pottstown's halcyon years came after World War II, just as other communities were flourishing. Industry burgeoned, and new industrial enterprises came to Pottstown. With them came executives of high caliber to lend knowledge, enterprise and leadership to civic endeavors. The walls of provincialism crumbled. No longer was Pottstown a sleepy small town.

High wages, promulgated during labor unions' organizational campaigns, sparked prosperity. Community services expanded. Urban redevelopment was begun to rebuild parts of the town.

There was a rebirth of municipal enterprises, because of the fertile imagination and indefatigable energy of a new borough manager, Robert H. McKinney. He served for almost a decade, between 1956 and 1965, years in which Pottstown made most progress.

Fervent activity was generated in rebuilding the town's water system, a $6-million job that made Pottstown the only municipality in the East that softened its water. The sewage treatment system was rebuilt. The municipal airport was expanded. Streets were reconstructed, and new ones built so that the community could boast that the day of the dirt road was passed. The municipal government actually was rebuilt to make it more pliable.

FUND-RAISING always was a prominent part of Shandy Hill's life. Here he is with Mayor Robert Briscoe, of Dublin, Ireland, at a Jewish rally in Pottstown for the sale of Israeli bonds.

Never had Pottstown seen so much activity, and the enterprise made an impression on contiguous townships, which set out to refurbish their communities too.

McKinney worked closely with the newspaper and appreciated its cooperation. Of this working relationship, he said:

"Perhaps the most important ingredient contributing to the progress of Pottstown's 'golden years' was the stimulus provided by The Pottstown Mercury. It was The Mercury's willingness and desire to exert its influence among the community leaders and in the many realms of community life that inspired community-wide support. Shandy Hill's personal efforts to overcome public apathy and, at times, partisan opposition, assured the success of many endeavors which otherwise would have failed. This aspect of positive newspaper involvement alone was of inestimable dimension in Pottstown's success story. Congratulations to you for your important contribution to the era of Pottstown's renaissance. It was a distinct personal privilege to have worked closely with you during those years."

* * * * *

During this period, too, Pottstown became well-known nationally because of its progressive newspaper. The "Big Story" on radio and television told millions of listeners and viewers of the crusading small-town newspaper, "the kind of paper William Allen White called the backbone of American journalism."

Pottstown became known because of the many national awards that came The Mercury's way: The National Fire Underwriters award of a gold medal and $500 for safety, the National Conference of Catholics and Jews brotherhood award, citations by universities, an award for its coverage of religion by the National Council of Religious Writers.

Soon a path was being beaten to Pottstown by students and groups anxious to observe its model government, or wanting to know what made the newspaper tick. Graduate students wrote theses on Pottstown's government. Out-of-state newspapers proposed they send their staffers to The Mercury for internships.

One of the highlights of this inquisitiveness came when a group of three government workers from the East African nation of Somalia, studying public administration at American University in Washington under United States sponsorship, came to Pottstown for a weeklong look at its way of life.

Washington knew about Pottstown. And the State Department also selected Pottstown when a large group of Latin-American trade unionists was touring the East. Frank Walling, of the United States State Department, shepherded the Latin-Americans through The Mercury offices.

"The Mercury is the only newspaper visited during this tour," he said. "It was selected as typical of the outstanding newspaper in America."

Of Pottstown, he declared: "It is a city with civic pride, and one reason it has civic pride is because it has a newspaper like The Mercury."

Chapter 10

SUFFER THE LITTLE ONES

Pennhurst State School, largest of Pennsylvania's hospitals for the mentally retarded, is on the fringe of Pottstown. It long had come under the critical eye of The Mercury because it was overcrowded, some hospital attendants criticized it for cruelty and others said it was a fire hazard.

The Mercury repeated these charges, but never got to the roots of its deplorable conditions because newsmen weren't welcome. Shandy Hill fretted for years about getting the facts out into the open, hoping the searchlight of publicity might alleviate them.

But how to get a reporter into the institution? One way, he thought, was to infiltrate the hospital with an attendant, for this type of employee always was needed.

He envisioned "training" a reporter as a male nurse at a nearby mental institution and having the attendant transfer to Pennhurst. Many attendants were floaters anyway, he mused, and it would be easy to make the switch. But death intervened. The state employee with whom he conspired died.

Hill's reporting instincts won over his attempt at subterfuge. Why not start at the top? So he went to Dr. Leopold A. Potkonski, Pennhurst superintendent, to suggest a sympathetic exposé in order to get help for the institution. Dr. Potkonski was extremely cooperative. He said he'd go along with the idea so long as The Mercury protected the identities of the unfortunate patients.

The exposé was an eye-opener to the entire state. A series of stories was so startling that a group of eleven influential legislators was induced to visit the "snakepit." They came to Pennhurst on their own time and at their own expense, and found conditions so shocking that they agreed relief had to come at once.

It was the first time many of the lawmakers ever had visited a state mental hospital. Weird sounds from the patients, the oppressive stench and sight of their personal torture caused the group to beg Dr. Potkonski to show them no more of the overcrowded, understaffed facility.

They left, vowing they'd remedy conditions.

They came back, along with the state Secretary of Welfare and a blue ribbon committee he appointed. The committee included legislators and officials of the Pennsylvania Association for Retarded Children.

In the meantime, the legislative leader called a conference of newspapermen in the capital, to outline conditions exposed by The Mercury. He enlisted the newspapermen's aid to carry the fight into all parts of the state. He had the Legislature appoint committees to visit each of the 29 state schools and hospitals.

This unprecedented personal visitation program resulted in a 70-page report to the Legislature and concomitant speedup in the state program to construct new hospital facilities and renovate old ones.

The firsthand knowledge obtained by the hospital panels resulted in the Mental Health Law of 1966, in which Pennsylvania affirmed its commitment to care for the mentally ill and retarded, and listed as its objective a meaningful life for every citizen who could be helped by medical and technical advances available.

It brought immediate $1.1-million relief to Pennhurst.

And the exposé brought a special resolution honoring The Mercury for its efforts in disclosing the distress of the mentally retarded at Pennhurst. This rare resolution was passed unanimously by the Pennsylvania House.

*　*　*　*　*

Assigned to the Pennhurst series was Andrew D. Cook, a

young staffer with little previous investigative experience. He followed his instructions so well and wrote so graphically that immediate public sympathy was aroused.

In his opening story, Cook said: "The Pennhurst State School is a nightmare, a grotesque dream that needn't exist.

"It's peopled by crippled and deformed figures. It abounds with clutching hands reaching out at nothing. It's filled with crooked mouths uttering wordless sounds.

"It's unavoidably dirty. It's overcrowded. It's understaffed. Rehabilitation and training programs are lost in the shuffle of 3,100 mentally retarded patients.

"Pennhurst, which strives to improve conditions of the mentally retarded, is relegated to the role of custodian of the backward."

Cook continued:

"Pennhurst is depressing. People don't like to think about it. The public is appalled by the stench of the wards, overcrowded with 'crib cases.' The public is shocked by the sight of middle-aged patients who have never been out of their cribs, who have not learned to use toilets. The sight of a man rubbing fecal matter in his hair, lying in a crib with no pants to cover his nakedness, shrieking senselessly, offends the sensitivities.

"The odor of the crib ward is overpowering. It follows the visitor away from the Pennhurst grounds. He smells it for several days. He washes himself thoroughly, but the smell won't go away. The reeking odor of human waste, and the waste of human lives, refuses to give way to soap.

"The stench is in the mind of the visitor. Every time he breathes, he thinks of the pitiful patients in the cribs, little elevated from the vegetable state of existence. The visitor's ideals about the basic dignity of mankind are shaken. He sees men who aren't really men and wonders how this can happen today, with all the knowledge man has at his grasp."

Cook found 3,182 patients in a hospital designed to accommodate 2,100. There were 425 attendants, most of them women. The attendants' wages started at $62 a week.

* * * * *

The Mercury enlisted the aid of State Representative Edwin G. Holl, who resided close to Pottstown, to carry the fight to the state Capitol. Overwhelmed by Pennhurst conditions, when he accompanied Mercury staffers on a tour, Holl, a Republican, adroitly sought the help of Democrats, then in power in the Legislature. He first won over Lester K. Fryer, a Democratic legislator from a nearby community, and then K. LeRoy Irvis, Democratic whip from Pittsburgh. They agreed to a personal trip to Pennhurst, at their own expense and on their own time.

Gordon P. Griffiths, another Mercury staffer, was assigned to follow the Pennhurst story and to make the trip with eleven state representatives from all parts of Pennsylvania who responded to the widely-publicized Mercury articles.

Reporting that they were "heartsick and dazed," he wrote: "They went away voicing their shock at what they saw in the overcrowded, understaffed facilities. If money can buy improvements, they will become Pennhurst ambassadors in the corridors at Harrisburg to see more money is appropriated at once, they declared.

"The impression was so great on their minds," Griffiths wrote, "that they asked what they could do as individuals, aside from being public servants, to help the men, women and children who inhabit the outdated wards."

"It is simply unbelievable to me what I have seen here," said Irvis, leader of the contingent. "The question ought not to be how much money we must spend, but how quickly we can provide it."

Mrs. Jane M. Alexander, a York lawyer and legislator, did not wish to be spared the sickening sights of the worse wards. At one point, she dampened her fingers with a fragrant oil and rubbed it to her nose to remove the overpowering odor of the helpless patients.

80

Representative Irvis, a Pittsburgh lawyer, knew how to get newspaper support throughout the state. After complete coverage in The Mercury, he called a press conference in Harrisburg. There the story went out over press association wires, and many dailies followed the leads as they developed.

Likewise, The Mercury exposé and wire reports drew much editorial attention. One of the most lucid and hard-hitting was an editorial in Pittsburgh's Pennsylvania Catholic, entitled "Shame on All of Us." It said:

"It is to the shame of each of us in Pennsylvania that conditions still exist in our mental hospitals such as those recently exposed at Pennhurst. A series of stories in The Pottstown Mercury revealed the pitiful picture: some 3,200 mentally retarded crowded into space designed for 2,200; filthy quarters; a hopelessly small staff; wards where patients sit naked and idle all day in a stark room, waiting simply for the hour to return to bed.

"These patients are naked because they tear off their clothes without adequate supervision; they are idle because there is no rehabilitation program, although many could be rehabilitated. Other patients, adult in body but so retarded mentally they can neither walk nor talk, spend their entire time in enlarged cribs, again without any hope of therapy, although some could profit from it . . . .

"Although the shame of Pennhurst falls on every Pennsylvanian, it lies heavier, we suggest, on the members of the State Legislature, most of whom have never been inside the institution, although, as legislators, they are responsible ultimately for the type of service which the institute provides. It required The Mercury to acquaint them with the situation.

"In view of the 'snake pit' conditions so often exposed in such institutions, one would think that periodic inspections of these state establishments would be a routine part of every legislator's schedule; obviously they are not.

"Promises for corrective action at Pennhurst have come from a number of legislators who toured the facility after

The Mercury stories appeared. K. Leroy Irvis, the Democrat from Pittsburgh's Hill District, said first steps have been taken for a new institution with a $1-million appropriation rushed through in the last week of the 1965 Legislature.

"But much more can be done, particularly today, than is being done at Pennhurst. It will require staff and funds, however, and these will require a sustained public interest. We who have recently established a record for self-indulgent Christmas spending can scarcely plead lack of funds. And if we really believe in the ideals of human dignity and Christian charity that we profess, then we cannot succumb to lack of interest."

* * * * *

Within two months State Secretary of Welfare Arlin M. Adams won overwhelming bipartisan support for his $1.1-million emergency fund for Pennhurst State School.

At the same time, a steering committee was appointed by the speaker of the House to create 29 subcommittees, one for each mental hospital and training school. During the summer and fall of 1966, they made their visits and prepared their findings and recommendations.

It was remarkable that nearly 50 percent of the House membership participated and all but two subcommittees reported as directed—the findings in many cases shockingly alike, even though the institutions were widely separated geographically.

The committee agreed that the most significant contribution of the visitations was the awareness it brought to lawmakers. Until they saw the conditions of the institutions across the state, it was the first visit ever for many, and they had been unaware of the full extent of Pennsylvania's mental illness and retardation challenge.

The committees recommended a number of changes reflecting legislative consciousness of a responsibility to become more closely and personally involved in care of the mentally deprived. A resume said: "They daringly opened a Pandora's box, and caught a fleeting, frightening—but enlightening—glimpse of the shadowy problems that abound within. They have pledged that though the struggle may continue with meager, uncertain resources and occasional bureaucratic confusion, it will no longer be logged down by legislative apathy."

* * * * *

The Legislature resolution commended The Mercury for its "crusade to assist the Pennhurst State School in making living conditions more tolerable for the patients who are confined there . . . . To The Mercury we say 'Thanks for bringing this condition to our attention.'

"Therefore, be it resolved that the General Assembly congratulates The Pottstown Mercury for its fine coverage of the conditions that prevailed at the Pennhurst School and for its untiring efforts in trying to correct them, and further be it resolved that copy of this resolution be forwarded to Shandy Hill, Andrew D. Cook and Gordon P. Griffiths, the reporters who so ably covered the story."

No similar resolution was known to have been adopted in the previous six sessions of the House.

The Mercury replied in kind with an editorial, "We Bow with Pride," which said:

"A newspaper never is any better than the quality of its local staff.

"The Mercury was honored many times for its public service. Its staff has an enviable national reputation for courage and resourcefulness, but few honors were as flattering as the resolution passed by the Pennsylvania Legislature. It praised The Mercury for its public service in crusading for better conditions at Pennhurst School.

"While The Mercury is flattered, its big reward will come when the unfortunately mentally deficient patients are given more humane treatment and better hospital surroundings. To

83

help the underprivileged and the unfortunate always has been an endeavor for this newspaper.

"We never have been content merely to publish the news. Our responsibility to you is far greater than that.

"The Mercury ever has been vigilant in its protection of the public interest. We believe both in exposing wrongdoing in the public realm and promoting the civic activities and forward-looking projects which advance the growth and development of our progressive community.

"A fearless and independent newspaper is your best safeguard against apathy and civic stagnation."

* * * * *

Two and a half years after The Mercury's Pennhurst exposé and subsequent commendation by the Legislature, the battle for betterment of conditions there was joined by two Philadelphia communications media.

The Philadelphia Inquirer, in July, 1968, published a series of stories exposing Pennhurst's vile conditions, and followed it with an editorial demand that the governor appoint a committee to investigate the charges.

At the same time, Philadelphia's WCAU radio and television stations "exposed" the lack of adequate supervisory help at Pennhurst and its crowded conditions. These stations likewise called editorially for relief.

The Inquirer admitted that "over the years there have been small armies of newsmen, cameramen, legislators and judges trooping through the place." The paper did not identify these "newsmen, cameramen and legislators," but added, "They have walked away sickened, appalled. Two years ago as a result of one such visit [This was the closest the newspaper came to naming the crusaders] the Legislature appropriated some $936,000 to improve the place. But the money didn't wind up at Pennhurst."

Chapter 11

FOR THE LEAST OF THESE

Depression's bind, long previous years of neglect and elected officials' false concept of economy left Pottstown's public school system in a sorry state of disrepair.

The school buildings, typical of the era, for the greater part were red brick squares, two stories high, without artificial light and without inside toilet facilities. All 17 were erected before the turn of 1900—and sadly outmoded.

Beams were of wood. The shoulder-high wainscotted corridors and cloakrooms were dry as tinder. The stairwells were deep and drafty. The wood stairs were oil-saturated to keep down the dust. The furnishings were all wooden.

The buildings were hot-air heated by antiquated "boilers" in the basements, close to the winter's coal supplies.

An 83-year-old firetrap was being used as a school for mentally retarded children.

The school buildings were fire hazards of the greatest concern, but old-line politicians failed to make reforms. The fire marshal complained he made inspections, pointed out hazards, made recommendations but they were never acted on by the school directors.

*　　*　　*　　*　　*

The Mercury pointed out the dangerous conditions, but not until 1938 was some improvement made. The political complexion of the school board had changed and a new group, led by Lawrence Orgill, an industrialist, responded to an "educational" campaign by The Mercury, and began to make changes. The public, alerted to the growing needs for improvement, showed no great concern when taxes were increased.

Some of the sorrier grade school buildings were eliminated and replaced by new structures. But not until a disastrous fire in 1949 razed a high school annex, converted from an 1890-vintage building, was Pottstown alerted to the need for school reform.

While firemen were still probing the $100,000 Richards School fire, The Mercury began an aggressive fire hazard campaign. This campaign revealed that kerosene lanterns still were used in some schools, that paint and shellac were stored beneath the dry wooden classroom floors. Flues were un-insulated. There was danger in every old building.

The Mercury widened its campaign to include firetraps in apartment houses and business establishments. The revelations were astonishing, indicating need for fire escapes, for cleanup in stores downtown that piled waste paper in basements, for fire extinquishers and for a building renewal program for the entire school district.

Such complete cooperation was obtained from school and borough officials that The Mercury undertook to write a stringent fire ordinance for Pottstown. No adequate law was on the borough's books.

Frank J. Dostal, later to become one of the news executives of the Rochester, N. Y., Times-Union, became engrossed in this project. He gathered samples of laws from fire underwriters. He worked around the clock—24 hours without sleep—to write a new law. The law, containing 35,000 words, was passed by Pottstown Council in June, 1950.

*   *   *   *   *

Of it, Martin P. Casey, engineer of the Middle Department of Association of Fire Underwriters, said, "Pottstown has by far the best ordinance in the State." It was used later as a model for eight other communities.

The work did not go unnoticed nationally. The Mercury was awarded the National Fire Underwriters gold medal and $500 for "outstanding public service" in a competition among 32 newspapers, from Houston, New Haven, Worcester and other larger communities.

The National Fire Underwriters made complete checks before the award was made. Unlike some other contests, when clippings are used as a basis, the fire hazard people came to Pottstown to make personal inspections, stage personal interviews, and generally oversee the results.

Shandy Hill escorted a New York official on an inspection tour of the public school buildings.

He pointed out the dangers of fire, and accentuated his tour by taking the inspector into the loft of a grade school building that was almost 100 years old.

The two inched over exposed wooden beams, Hill pointing out how tinder-dry the beams were.

Suddenly Hill slipped and fell, his right foot puncturing the dry-as-dust brittle plaster. The leg penetrated the ceiling in the schoolroom below, and sprinkled the classroom with dust. The lesson was interrupted, but none of the pupils was injured.

There was no damage, except for the small hole in the ceiling.

A short few days thereafter, Hill got a $69.20 bill from the school district for plastering repairs.

Chapter 12

POLICE REFORM

If ever reform was needed, it was in the Pottstown Police Department—for the protection of the public as well as for the protection of the policeman.

This was high on the list of The Mercury's crusades. Achievement came slowly, but crusades took the police out of politics and gave them civil service protection. The watchful eye of The Mercury ended petty police graft. The biggest benefit was law enforcement.

The newspaper's greatest achievement in this field was a decision to hire a professional for head of the department, a professional chosen by an impartial professional firm after a nationwide search and close written and oral examinations.

This did more to improve the caliber of police protection than any other improvement innovated. It also improved the caliber of police employee, and attracted dedicated men and women to law enforcement work.

* * * * *

An observant editor, interested in public service, could not overlook the great need for extensive reform in the police department.

In the 1930's the police chief and all his patrolmen were political appointees. They needed no qualifications. They were friends of a councilman or "good guys who needed jobs"!

When the political complexion of council changed, the chief and his men could be turned out—and usually were.

Policemen needed no formal education; in fact, one police officer in 1931 could neither read nor write. Knowledge of the law was not a requisite; that came later, if at all, for policemen those days had few duties to perform and made few or no arrests.

One Pottstown policeman confided to Shandy Hill that he had made only one arrest in his career.

"That was during World War I," he recounted. "During those days, when a man deserted the Army, there'd be a $25 reward for the policeman who turned him in.

"I was broke, and I knew Joe Blank went over the hill. I also knew where he was swimming that day. So I went to the swimming hole and picked him up.

"I'm sorry I gotta pinch you," the policeman told him, "but I need the money."

That was his record.

*   *   *   *   *

The worst aspect was that Pottstown never got any trained police. The Mercury pointed out frequently that new appointees bought uniforms, were handed badges and guns and turned out on the street. They'd be told what beat to walk, and that was that.

There were few checks on the police, if any. They didn't report to the police station if they didn't feel like it. It was hard to find a policeman at night, unless the man on the street knew that one of the uniformed men would be in the Elks club at a certain time after midnight.

In fact, The Mercury became incensed when it learned the whole of Pottstown was left unprotected one night when four policemen (one less than the entire shift) obligingly acted as doormen at a popular "dressup" charity dance. The police opened automobile doors, escorted the guests into the club and then "guarded" the frolickers the remainder of the night. Only a deskman remained on duty in the police department that night.

No police docket was kept. Therefore there was no crime!

There was no graft to speak about, unless it was petty. The cop on the beat might ask a merchant for a white dress shirt—and usually got it.

There'd be the usual Christmas gifts of liquor, sometimes whole cases brought in to the chief to "share it with the boys." The "boys" or the rank and file of the department, knew about this, but they felt they weren't getting their just share. Policemen thought the chief stashed away most of the liquor in his private office.

There was some kind of poetic justice, then, when the chief's office was burglarized, and the choice liquor removed from his locker. Yet not one word of recrimination was uttered from the inner office.

The policeman blinked his eye at horse-race bookmaking joints, but only because the chief executives or the police chief allowed these joints to run. Here, as in other cities, law violation flourished because the police knew about it! Bookies walked unmolested from store to store in the business section every day, taking bets from merchants and clerks.

There was no rowdyism in the 1930s. Let a "prominent" citizen get drunk, and police most likely would drive him home. Crimes of passion were unheard of until the lush times of World War II, when plenty of money stimulated appetites for the forbidden.

The Mercury heard many reports that gamblers were making payoffs to someone in the police department. As in so many similar rumors, the usual "brown bag" containing the payoff was passed to an officer, these reports said. But The Mercury never was able to come up with evidence that graft was passed—at least not in city hall, where staffers were assigned to a 24-hour watch in the police department.

The Mercury hammered away for law enforcement, knowing fully that police laxity allows crime to flourish.

One of the newspaper's most determined campaigns was against a drinking place that developed into a brothel of a most repugnant nature. The place became acutely obnoxious when The Mercury reported that minor girls were sold liquor and then taken to upstairs rooms for assignation.

The publicity had no effect on the heads of the Pottstown police department, and the foot patrolmen would not act without orders.

Finally, the newspaper's din became so insistent that Judge E. Arnold Forrest, of the Montgomery County Court, ordered a cleanup. The Mercury headlined "Outside Enforcement Needed to Close House of Prostitution," but local officials never commented. The barroom's proprietor pleaded guilty and went to jail.

Judge Harold G. Knight, of the Montgomery County Court, commented, "This was a terrible situation—a public disgrace."

*　*　*　*　*

While the public received a small bit of protection, the policeman got none. In 1931 there were eleven in the police department—a chief and ten officers. When a Democratic council was defeated at the polls, the Republicans were likely to turn out the chief and men. The chief would get a job at a factory as a security policeman. The rank and file might take to grave-digging or sidewalk-repairing.

When a new chief of police was appointed, he might be a friend of the political leader or a relative of the head of the council's police committee. The Mercury, with the interest of the community and the policeman at heart, campaigned for police civil service. It took some campaigning. It took many stories to point out what little law enforcement was evident, how traffic tickets were fixed, how parking violators were excused.

It took many stories about bookmaking joints; even to publishing an affidavit by a horse-race house customer who swore that he embezzled $12,000 of his employer's funds to gamble, and lost it on the bangtails. The public disclosure didn't help him at his trial. He was sentenced to two years in prison.

Editorials pointed out that one prominent citizen committed suicide after losing all his money at a bookie shop. Another was alleged to have drunk himself to death in sorrow over his losings.

The ministerial association took up the cry. Pastors thundered from their pulpits. The Rev. E. S. Horn, a Lutheran, asked, "Why can't excessive gambling be stopped—gambling that has caused men to rot so they might continue to try to turn their luck, gambling which has caused men to commit suicide rather than face their shame?"

An investigative committee of five ministers interviewed police—and merely got the fisheye. The gambling wheels continued to spin.

There were stories on gambling rooms, where craps throwers competed from after midnight to dawn, and how a professional man had lost his bankroll backing a game. The stories told how professional gamblers "lugged" customers to Pottstown from cities 75 miles away for "fresh capital."

*   *   *   *   *

The Mercury declared stricter law enforcement would come if the police were not at the mercy of politicians. What police needed was protection as much as the public needed it, The Mercury said.

Shandy Hill expected no millenium, in which the gambler in sheep's clothing would lie down with the lion in uniform. But he did believe a better caliber of worker could be obtained through examination, not only of the applicant's intelligence or knowledge of the law and the community, but of his character as well.

The going was slow. Long pounding of the editorial anvil finally culminated in reform. On July 5, 1941, council passed a law creating a police civil service commission. In December of that year, examinations for policemen were given by the commission. These examinations have not ended all evils. But there has been improvement. Better police have been hired.

Then came a loud campaign to gain a professional policeman for the head of the department. Council approved the idea, hired an outside firm to recruit applications and to screen them. Long series of interviews were held, and in May, 1964, after a nationwide search, a professional, Milton David Hooper, of St. Petersburg, Florida, was hired. He took a better paying job with more opportunity in Roanoke, Virginia, in 1967. His successor, following another search, was Richard Tracy, a former Chicago police sergeant.

In 1968 there were 32 members of the police department. In 1931, the payroll was $20,154 a year, in 1968, the payroll was $188,477.

Where once the police could be turned out on the streets without recourse, without cause, Pottstown's police now have fairly high wages and civil service protection, good pensions, vacations and other benefits, all because the daily newspaper was interested in their welfare and was willing to front for them.

As for the community, it has greater respect for its professional police!

Chapter 13

A DECISION FROM HIGH

Time, the weekly newsmagazine, headed the story: "WARNING TO PIRATES."

Then it said: "Nothing is more certain to send an editor through the roof than to see his exclusive stories turn up without credit . . . on a local radio station's newscast. The practice is so widespread and so deep rooted in tradition that most editors do no more about it.

"One who did was Managing Editor Shandy Hill of Pennsylvania's Pottstown Mercury, who was irked for years by what he claimed was the lifting of his news by a local broadcaster. After a long battle with Pottstown's WPAZ, Hill has the satisfaction of a Pennsylvania Supreme Court ruling affirming that news is the property right of those who gather it, and pirates can be punished."

Time was right. Newspapermen continually griped about "theft" of their news. Some did more to stop the filching. But in Pennsylvania none ever asked the courts for legal restrictions.

Some copyrighted the news. So did The Mercury. But the others, like The Mercury, found the copyright didn't act as a deterrent.

It was not this way everywhere, Walter Lister, late managing editor of the Philadelphia Bulletin, told Hill, "The only news we copyright is the local news. Why? To keep the radio stations from picking it up. The copyright at least makes them think. There is such a thing as ethics, and they don't pick up the news without permission."

E. Z. Dimitman, one of the most brilliant of Pennsylvania journalists, who was then managing editor of The Philadelphia Inquirer, said the same day: "I am rubbed the wrong way when I hear a radio station say, 'The prize news today is,' and then it treats as brand new a story that was at least twelve hours old before it even appeared in The Inquirer that morning."

*   *   *   *   *

The Mercury laid some traps, some rather blatant pitfalls, rather than the adroit temptations that William Randolph Hearst tossed in the path of his arch rival Joseph Pulitzer, in the days of the Spanish-American War, before the turn of the century.

Then Hearst's Journal was slugging it out for circulation supremacy with Pulitzer's World; a battle of two sensational penny papers. Hearst accused Pulitzer of pilfering the news, but he had no tangible evidence until the Journal invented a Colonel Reflipe W. Thenuz, "an Austrian artillerist of European renown," who died in the war zone.

The World fell into the trap. When it picked up the item about Col. Reflipe W. Thenuz, The Journal admitted the subterfuge and charged, in substance, "Rearrange those letters in the Colonel's name and you come up with 'We pilfer the news'! "

After hearing radio announcers read The Mercury's local news word for word, the newspaper planned some pitfalls. The Mercury's counsel employed a private detective agency to make tape recordings of radio newscasts. Then The Mercury published an outrageous item, and buried it well inside the paper. The radio announcer read it word for word.

*   *   *   *   *

The Mercury's counsel twice asked the radio station to discontinue the pilfering. Twice promises to cease were made, but the practice was not stopped. The pickup without attribution was continued, and The Mercury's counsel compiled a long list of stories appropriated without so much as confirmation.

Finally the breaking point came, and the paper filed suit to enjoin Pottstown Broadcasting Company, operator of radio station WPAZ, from "pirating the local news articles from The Pottstown Mercury."

The Mercury asked merely for an injunction. It did not seek punitive damages.

In its complaint, The Mercury alleged that it had a property right in the news which it gathered, edited and published. Up to this time, no such property rights had been established in Pennsylvania law. It further recited that the local news items had been copyrighted, and notice had appeared on the masthead of the paper.

The Mercury's counsel, William A. O'Donnell, Jr., based his claim for relief on the fact that "both the newspaper and radio station disseminate news to the same general area and sell advertising within the same area.

The newspaper, he said, spends considerable money "to develop its sources of local news, train personnel, and to accurately and concisely compose local news items." Such specialized treatment of the local news was the principal factor in its circulation and sale of advertising.

The radio station, the suit said, "has without license, permission, or authority . . . on numerous occasions in the past and is so continuing in the present to use the local news stories . . . for its own broadcast of news.

Such unauthorized use, the complaint continued, "violates the property rights of the plaintiff."

*　　*　　*　　*　　*

The suit was filed in Montgomery County Court in 1960.

Long delays came, and depositions were not taken until 1962. Finally, the case was placed on the court calendar and trial was begun on January 2, 1963. Only Hill was placed on the stand, and after a few preliminary questions relating to the operation of the newspaper, the radio station's counsel challenged the county court's jurisdiction in the case.

Judge Daniel L. Quinlan, Jr., agreed to a postponement and suggested that the court *en banc* hear argument. Within two weeks, the entire court upheld Judge Quinlan's denial to dismiss the case for lack of jurisdiction.

The broadcasting company appealed to the state Supreme Court, saying, "It is impossible to copyright a news item per se" and that the newspaper "does not have property rights in the 'local news items.' " The denial continued: "Local news items are an item of public domain, and the defendant has the right to use them upon its news broadcasting as it sees fit."

In a decision dated July 23, 1963, the Pennsylvania Supreme Court decided many of the issues. The Court's seven justices agreed unanimously that local news items gathered by a newspaper's reporters are the property of that newspaper, and unauthorized use by a radio station is unfair competition and a violation of a property right.

Further, the high court said, "If the news company can establish by proof that the broadcasting company, has, without authority, used the local news item gathered through specialized methods and by the trained personnel of the news company, such unauthorized use constitutes a violation of a property right."

Justice Benjamin B. Jones wrote the decision, covering a wide field. He said:

"In this day and age, no court can fail to take note of the fact that newspapers, radio and television stations compete with each other for advertising, which has become a giant in our economy. In fact, the presentation of news and entertainment has become almost a subsidiary function of newspapers, radio and television stations; advertising is the lifeblood of newspapers, radio and television and the presentation of news by all three media is a service to attract advertisers.

"Taking into consideration the circumstances and the character of the businesses of the respective parties, as

97

averred, the news company has a commercial package of news items to service its advertising business upon which to have a cause of action against a competitor allegedly converting the news items to its own uses in pursuit of advertising. The distinction we draw is fine; for the purpose of an action of unfair competition the specialized treatment of news items as a service the newspaper provides for advertisers gives to the news company a limited property right which the law will guard and protect against wrongful invasion by a competitor. . . .

"Competition in business is jealously protected by the law, and the law abhors that which tends to diminish or stifle competition. While a competitor may, subject to the patent, copyright and trademark laws, imitate his rival's business practices, processes and methods, yet the protection which the law affords to competition does not and should not countenance the usurpation of a competitor's investment and toil. . . . If the news company can establish by proof that the broadcasting company has, without authority, used the local news items gathered through the specialized methods and by the trained personnel of the news company, such unauthorized use constitutes a violation of a property right."

If the broadcasting company has "pirated" news items, the decision continued, that "states a violation of a property right and a claim of unfair competition which the state courts have jurisdiction to determine."

*   *   *   *   *

The broadcasting company did not rest here. It appealed its case to the Federal Court, based on involvement of the copyright laws, but Federal Judge Ralph C. Body refused to accept jurisdiction in the "news piracy case."

Not that he was deciding the copyright issue, Judge Body said, but he returned the case to the county courts because the broadcasting station's removal petition to send the case to Federal Court was filed after a twenty-day limit. The broadcasting company was ordered to pay all costs, counsel fees and other disbursements in connection with the attempt to have the case brought to Federal Court.

The Mercury did not press the matter further. The newspaper believed it had won its big point; that there is a property right to news, and that proof of unfair competition is actionable.

" 'This is a boon to every newspaperman who has his stuff swiped,' " Time quoted Hill as saying. " 'This lifting of stories was just like getting my pocket picked.' "

* * * * *

The Pennsylvania Supreme Court decision created a flurry of interest when the Associated Press (which itself had won an unfair competition case against International News Service in the U.S. Supreme Court) distributed the story over its wires. Editor and Publisher, trade journal of the newspaper profession, reported the case in full.

This brought a host of inquiries to lawyer O'Donnell from all over the United States. They asked: How did you do it? May we have copies of your briefs?

Newspapers from Massachusetts to California, aggrieved by similar radio troubles, flooded O'Donnell with so many questions that he had all the briefs and court records reprinted and sent them to the inquirers.

One of the first dailies to follow The Mercury's lead was the Madisonville, Ky., Messenger. This newspaper filed a suit in 1966 against its local radio station, charging it with news piracy. The newspaper said radio station WFMW, "without permission, used and broadcast as its own many of the news stories and items compiled and gathered by the plaintiff and published in its afternoon newspaper."

Hopkins Circuit Judge C. J. Waddill issued a permanent injunction against the radio station, restraining it from using in any manner, or broadcasting over the radio station WFMW for a period of 20 hours after the publication of the plaintiff's newspaper (The Messenger)."

This was the first case of its kind in Kentucky. The

Messenger said it was "one which had attracted wide attention within both newspaper and broadcasting circles all across the nation."

Chapter 14

SCHOOL FOR JOURNALISTS

Because The Pottstown Mercury was so well known, it attracted many applicants for editorial staff positions. Not all of these young men and women were "graduated" from Shandy Hill's School of Journalism. Some quickly learned they were better fitted for selling insurance or strawberry festival tickets. Only a small amount of mediocrity found its way into the newsroom.

The job of training was difficult, but the pace never got so fast that Shandy Hill was unable to give personal attention to each individual staffer. The rewards outweighed the grief. Not all pupils of "The School" were graduated into big-league newspaper competition, but so many went on to brilliant metropolitan papers that the name of The Mercury became legendary.

"If you've worked on The Mercury, you've got it," wrote Frank Dostal, star reporter of the period right after the end of World War II. Dostal, night editor of the Rochester, N.Y., Times-Union writes here:

"I broke in on The Mercury.

"Six simple little words. Yet to those who know newspapers and newspapering, they are enough.

"They are a cachet; a sort of invisible badge that says:

"By God, if this guy was good enough to make it there, he's a NEWSPAPERMAN!'

"For an eager cub, who had dreamed of being a reporter from the time he put out his own handprinted newspaper as a kid, there was no better place to start. Part of it was youth; part of it was the town, but most of it was Shandy Hill.

"From the first day you started—when he told you, 'If it's news, write it!'—to the day you left—when he said, 'We can't compete with the big leagues'—he was always there—driving, driving, driving.

"Inevitably, you alternately loved him and hated him, sometimes one more than the other, but you *worked* for him. When you got a scathing note because you had goofed in a story, you could curse him so bitterly the girls in the society department would blush—but you didn't make that mistake again. When your assignment sheet noted that that morning's stories were 'dandy' or 'ginger peachy' (and where did a hard case like Shandy get those expressions?) you hoarded it. (In fact, some still are tucked away in our attic.)

* * * * *

"It was not until you were older that you wondered how he could have enough faith in a raw cub to assign him to the Mimi Green murder case, possibly the most sensational in the history of the state, with the simple instruction: 'Cover it.'

"And cover it The Mercury did. From the day the body was discovered until the end of the trial, few readers ever knew the effort that went into it. But The Mercury's readers often knew things about the case before the official investigators did—a situation that led District Attorney Frederick B. Smillie (later to become a judge) to accuse its reporters of impersonating police officers to get information (we didn't).

"The trial was an endurance test of its own. Five eighteen-hour days with a photographer running a taxi service to Norristown because the reporter couldn't drive; Sports Editor Bob Riegner hauling quart bottles of beer from Pomerey Lucci's Bar on High Street to quench a seemingly insatiable thirst, and City Editor Chuck Treleven ripping copy from the typewriter as fast as it could be written to fill pages and pages of type.

"A year later, Pottstown readers learned how thorough that coverage had been when the Pennsylvania Newspaper Publishers Association voted The Mercury first prize for court coverage—over every paper in the state. And three years later, Erle Stanley Gardner's 'Court of Last Resort' was using that information to help win freedom for Gerald Wentzel, who had been convicted of the crime.

*　*　*　*　*

"But Shandy Hill's pride in his staff was short-lived (or so it seemed to us). He kept driving us on. How do you choose from among a host of memories? Well, consider these:

"—The night Justice of the Peace Dick Cadmus, blind and ill, traded Biblical quotations with a street corner evangelist, matching him chapter and verse despite his handicap, and sent him to jail (the story of that encounter won another award for The Mercury).

"—The casual way Shandy Hill, after a series of disastrous fires, said, 'What we need is a new fire ordinance. Write it.' That took days of research into the best ordinances in the country, a 24-hour typing job on the part of three persons, and personal delivery of mimeographed copies into the hands of the fire committee of borough council. It passed virtually unchanged and gave Pottstown its first up-to-date fire code in years (the National Fire Underwriters thought so highly of it they awarded The Mercury their gold medal that year).

"—And, long before civil rights became such a burning issue, The Mercury took up the cause of the Negro families on Cottage and Hemlock Rows, threatened by the loss of their homes by the powerful Federal Government.

" 'It's unjust,' Shandy said. 'Fight them.'

"A solid thirty-day campaign mobilized the support of churches, unions, businessmen, industry and some powerful behind-the-scenes allies, and the U.S. Housing Authority gave up (that battle for the right of Negroes to own their own homes won yet another award—for public service—years before the Supreme Court acted in 1954).

"Reporters learned on the job that the power of the press—especially in The Mercury's case—was no myth. Once, at the request of the Pennsylvania State Publishers' Associa-

103

tion, we totaled the number of campaigns conducted by the newspaper over the preceding 24 months. The score: 41 won, six continuing, two lost!

"The two losses were a 'day' for baseball pitcher Bobby Shantz and a 'dinner' for the town's championship women's softball team. To those of us on the staff they didn't rate as 'campaigns,' but Shandy included them anyway. And he never could understand how they failed in a sportsloving town—perhaps wishful thinking on the part of an old sports editor.

"But not all the memories were of awards.

"For one reporter, they include such things as:

"—Regularly burglarizing Police Chief James A. Laughead's office to get crime reports ('Get the story,' Shandy said, and we got it).

"—The night Burgess William A. Griffith and Councilman J. Max Creswell called Chuck Treleven to ask the character of a reporter going with a Pottstown girl (he married her, has three children—and with no help from Shandy).

"—The day an excited Shandy called about a wildcat walk-out at the Jacobs Aircraft plant. 'Don't shave, wear your oldest clothes, look as if you worked on the production line and *SNEAK* into that union meeting and find out what's going on,' he directed. As the reporter walked down the steps into the basement meeting room in the Singer building, he was greeted on all sides. Many of the workers were fellow members of the Empire Hook and Ladder Company ('Get the trust of your contacts and don't lose it,' Shandy had warned). For three days, the reporter attended every union meeting, and at the end of the walkout, introduced himself to the union president who did not know he had been there. He was thanked for the objectivity of The Mercury's coverage.

"—And, finally, the day Police Sgt. Tommy Lawler came into the Mercury with a farewell gift of cigarettes and a lighter ('Treat everyone fairly,' Shandy had admonished).

The cigarettes have long gone up in smoke, but the lighter, battered and scarred, still is a well-used and proud possession.

"How well did Shandy train his reporters?

"Perhaps the final accolade came from Paul Miller, president of the Associated Press and publisher of The Rochester, N.Y., Democrat and Chronicle where this reporter now works. Purely by chance I saw my application for a job. Across one corner Miller had written to the late George Shoals, managing editor:

" 'George: Hire this man. The paper he comes from is one of the best of its kind in the country.'

"—Yes, I broke in on The Mercury."

Chapter 15

HIS FAVORITE DAY

Every staffer who toiled in The Mercury's vineyard over the past 37 years had a different memory of the days when he was taught "getting out a newspaper is 90 percent fun." Of course, it wasn't all fun; there was much drudgery, as on every newspaper.

But the tyro learned there were no reasons why a small-town newspaper could not be aggressive, interesting, well written and even more reliable and better edited than its big neighbors. That's why The Mercury could compete with the metropolitans.

The neophyte enjoyed working for a paper in which he had pride. He was happy to share in putting out a good product, and many of the red-blooded youths who survived the daily rigors went on to star-studded careers.

Barry Nemcoff, who came "cold" to The Mercury, went on to other newspapers, TV news, United States Information Service in Europe and Asia, then back into communications as news director of WCAU-TV in Philadelphia.

* * * * *

His memory? The editor's edict to "get the story" takes tenacity and leaves an indelible impression. He tells his story, "One of My Favorite Reminiscences of Days at The Mercury," here:

"The slip of paper was on top of the desk—face down. Nothing new, really. You always found them face down when reporting for your shift at the Pottstown Mercury.

"This was your daily assignment slip, and after making a great pretense that it wasn't there at all, you went through the ritual of looking to see what was on it. Normally, if you

106

found a piece of paper on your desk lying face down, you would merely turn it over to see what was written on it when you knew there was something written on it.

"But at The Mercury, the fact that Shandy Hill was responsible for its contents made the difference. You knew that the managing editor had spent all afternoon pondering its contents before setting down the typewritten words in the cryptic style only veterans of The Mercury newsroom could decipher.

"Figuring out what it said was the 'fun' part. It was that other—executing the managing editor's orders—that was the agony.

"No wonder most reporters turned up the facedown slip much as they would a draw card in poker. This was a hand in which the stakes were high indeed.

"It was a hot, muggy day in August, 1952, long before editorial rooms in small-town newspapers were air-conditioned. Definitely not the kind of day for appreciation of the unknown. It was the kind of day when there would be more concern for the perspiration under your shirt than for events shaping Pottstown during the current 24 hours.

"Little wonder that I turned up my assignment sheet a few minutes after six in the evening with more than the usual trepidation. Of course, my fears were soon justified. Among other things, I was being ordered out into the hot evening to interview an oldtimer supposed to be celebrating his one-hundredth birthday the next day.

"After confirming with Ed Rosenberg, the news editor on duty, that the trip was absolutely essential (an exercise in desperation, since I knew what his reply would be), I set out.

*   *   *   *   *

"Fortunately, the walk to the oldtimer's house was a short one. And that's where my dubious luck ran out. After repeated knocking at the door, I heard the shuffling sound of footsteps on the other side. An elderly woman opened the door.

"She looked worn, very worn and hot. Looking at her thin, sharp face, it did not take much to guess that the last thing she wanted to do was speak with a young newspaper reporter. And the first thing I wanted to do was to oblige her, but there was the *assignment.* And an assignment from Shandy Hill was not to be taken lightly, regardless of its nature. In short, you either got the story or began looking for a new job, in an era when the fifty-dollars-a-week I was getting as a cub reporter represented the height of good fortune for aspiring beginners.

" 'What do you want?'

"Her tone confirmed my first impression of her. I could see she was ready to slam the door in my face before giving me an opportunity to state my business. The apparent desperation in my eyes must have saved me.

"As briefly as I could, I told of the reason for my call. Her reply was equally brief; her brother was too ill to see anyone, least of all talk to anyone, especially about the secret of his success to having managed to live one hundred years.

"I was elated—super-elated, if there is such a word. 'Off the hook,' I thought as I rapidly retraced my steps to The Mercury in anticipation of spending the rest of the evening in the newsroom gathering stories by phone.

"On a hot night, small blessings can become exaggerated. But, I soon found out my joy was premature. There was little expression of sympathy on Rosenberg's face as I told him about the oldtimer's ill health precluding the possibility of a 'happy birthday' story.

* * * * *

"After what I felt was a long and reasonable explanation, the news editor merely asked, 'What's the assignment say?'

" 'To get the story, but . . . .'

"He appeared pained by my stupidity. 'He's going to be a hundred tomorrow, isn't he?'

" 'I guess so, but his sister says he can't talk to anyone,' in a last ditch attempt.

108

" 'Go,' he said. And I went the three blocks back to the oldtimer's home.

"Of course, it was more difficult this time. The worn woman was less sharp, but much more persuasive. She took the time to tell the young reporter at her door that her brother had been bedridden for years, that he was senile, that he was often incoherent, that he had to be handled like a helpless child.

"Armed with these facts, surely the argument against doing a story about the oldtimer's prescription for longevity was indisputable. Or so I thought.

"Rosenberg was no more impressed by my second and longer recitation than he had been by my first. It's not that he lacked compassion. The fact is he worked for the same man I did, and to violate an assignment from Shandy Hill would have the same end result for him as it would for me— with my having the edge, since news editors always have been less marketable.

"There's no point in going over the exact words of the conversation that ensued between Rosenberg and me on my second return. Suffice it to say that on my third trip to the oldtimer's home, my heart was beating considerably faster, even if my walking pace was slower.

*　　*　　*　　*　　*

"I'm sure the old woman was just as surprised to see me there for the third time as I was to find myself there. On seeing me again, she made the mistake of assuming, for a fleeting moment, an expression that I interpreted for weakness before an assault. I pressed on. Putting all of the pain at my disposal into my face, I beseeched her. It was either an interview with her brother or my job. Simple as that.

"She did not assent immediately. She took time to weight the discomfort of the proposed interview to her spent brother against the needs of a career for a young man.

"The latter won out, and she replied by smiling for the

first time in our three encounters. It was the kind of smile of which I would have thought her incapable. The sharp, worn look disappeared; even the perspiration on her lined face seemed to dry up. There was a real freshness in it as she said, 'Maybe it's good that sometimes people don't give up easily. I've been like that most of my life, taking care of old Sam and all that.'

"The story didn't make the front page the next day, but it got into print. It told of an old, old man who, by rights, should have been dead long ago. It speculated on how he might be hanging on because of the tenacity of a tired sister's care. It didn't say anything about another man's insistence on tenacity.

"I think I may have learned something that evening."

Chapter 16

THE LUCK OF THE PRESENT

What dedicated young newspaperman never dreamed about his own big story?

Being assigned to the big disaster, to the race riot, to the flood or holocaust—such stories, bylined on Page One, bring their thrills and rewards.

But the imaginative day-dreaming newspaperman conjures up more than this. He must be the big part of the story. The main character in it!

It seldom happens. Sometimes a reporter is lucky enough to get stuck between floors in an office building elevator, and writes the human interest story of the rescue. Sometimes the bright young lad is taking his wife to a hospital for the birth of their first child, and the delivery takes place in his automobile.

The accounts spellbind readers. A gutsy writer can recount "How I Licked Cancer," and that will enthrall readers for a few days.

The odds are lopsided against even these events.

But to be a survivor of a marine disaster that took 134 lives; to have recovered from a six-hour ordeal after jumping into the cold stormy Atlantic Ocean, and to have lived to write the hero's story—what are the odds against that happening?

Agnes Prince, 29-year-old Mercury society editor, wrote her own story of living through the horrors of a pleasure ship's burning off the New Jersey coast.

A small-town newspaper, such as The Mercury, has to be "lucky" to get a break like this. But there's something about a genuine newspaperman being on the scene at the right time. Maybe this was it.

The Mercury was lucky to have been able to give Pottstown this story before the big-city newspapers broke the news. The Mercury did it with an "off time" extra.

*   *   *   *   *

The story broke on a Saturday, after The Mercury's morning edition had been circulated. The night report closed at 2 A.M. Teletypes were not running. They wouldn't come on again until Sunday noon.

It was September 8, 1934, close to noon. A couple of employees were sitting around, awaiting the noon hour to close the office, when Louis Prince, employee of a Pottstown furniture store, walked into the office.

"Did you hear anything from Agnes?" he asked excitedly about his sister. "How is she?"

"Why?"

"The *Morro Castle* burned, and Agnes was saved at sea," he blurted. "She just telephoned me. What can you find out about her?"

The Mercury knew, of course, that Miss Prince was on a vacation cruise to Havana on the *Morro Castle,* accompanied by her sister, Ruth, 22, and a family friend, Evelyn Henricks, also 22. The Mercury also knew the *Morro Castle,* of 11,520 tonnage, had a high safety rating and had 562 persons aboard (yet 134 perished).

Louis Prince was giving Shandy Hill what meager details he got in an unsatisfactory telephone conversation from Fitkin Hospital, in Asbury Park, N.J. His sister Ruth had been saved, too, but he knew nothing about the Henricks girl's whereabouts.

By now, Hill was on the telephone, asking the Associated Press in Philadelphia to give The Mercury what it had on the disaster and to switch on the teletypes.

This was before the efficient radio networks spilled news over the airways. It also was many years before the magic eye of on-the-scene television, which can kill a newspaper story.

So Hill decided to "extra"!

*   *   *   *   *

A few printers on the day shift still were in the composing room. Hill called in stereotypers and pressmen.

Then Hill risked a telephone call to Fitkin Hospital. He knew the place would be besieged by anxious families, so he put on his best professional tone and insisted it was a matter of life and death to speak to Agnes Prince. Since then, he has often pondered how childish that must have sounded.

But it worked. And Hill talked to Agnes. She could fill in only a few details because she still was overwrought and in shock. The little she said was enough to bolster a decision to get out an extra edition. The circulation department was alerted to get some boys to sell papers on the street.

AP gave The Mercury enough to write a seven-column, two-line boxcar type streamer: "3 Pottstown Girls Aboard Ocean Liner Hit by Lightning," with a three-line subhead shrieking "Report 300 lost as Liner Morro Castle Burns in Hurricane at Sea Off Asbury Park."

It was a fragmentary story and full of errors, as later facts developed. The account recited how the three Pottstown girls were on the liner, but it skirted exactitude except to say the trio was among "two boatloads of survivors landed at Asbury Park." This was Agnes' word, but it was incorrect.

The story said survivors were picked up by the liner *Monarch of Bermuda* and a freighter, *Andrew F. Luckenbach.* The freighter had rescued the Henricks girl and taken her to New York.

*   *   *   *   *

Other details included a parenthetical note that the *Morro Castle's* captain, Robert R. Wilemot, had died the night before the tragedy and that First Officer William F. Warms was in command. Because of later court trials, The Mercury was glad it injected those names into the first story.

The extra edition was nothing much to write home about, but it sold like the proverbial hotcakes.

113

Miss Prince told her bylined eye-witness story for the regular edition of Monday's Mercury. The Mercury also had bylined stories by Agnes's sister and Miss Henricks. Staffers wrote these.

The feature yarn, of course, was Miss Prince's. It told how a festive farewell party (the ship was only a few miles out of its New York destination) turned into a nightmare.

At 3:30 A.M. the Pottstown girl was alarmed by the odor of smoke. A telephone call brought the matter-of-fact reply: "Yes, there's a fire aboard. We're trying to locate it now."

Agnes awakened her sister. They tossed dressing robes over their shoulders and raced onto the deck. The ship was blazing. Smoke blinded them. Contrary to the order to remain calm, Agnes and Ruth climbed aboard a rail and jumped the frightening distance into the dark, murky seas far below.

"No movie, no story I ever read or heard, has quite caught the actual feeling of such a dread event," Miss Prince dramatically wrote in what must have been the year's greatest understatement.

And then came the newspaperman's credo:

"Throughout the ordeal, I kept thinking what a story this will make," she said.

Her description of her six hours in the dark waters was inspirational. Her plunge into the Atlantic was so deep she thought her lifejacket never would buoy her to the surface, but she remembered to hold her breath. Her lungs almost burst.

Finally she surfaced, able to see nothing, but to hear shouts around her. She yelled for "Ruthie." There was no answer for hours. Finally she was attracted to a light. It was merely a flare set off by a crew member, but her sister was attracted to it also, and they were reunited.

Daylight brought scores of rescue boats of all sizes, from fishing boats to large cruisers, to the scene of the disaster. A small fishing boat, the *Paramount*, hauled the Prince sisters aboard and landed them at Brielle, New Jersey. The Princes didn't learn until Sunday that Miss Henricks had been taken to New York aboard a freighter.

Agnes, in a low-key description of herself, told how "clad in a pair of shoes three sizes too large, a huge but warm coat and dress loaned to me by friends," she came back to Pottstown to return to work.

She saw nothing of a jinx in the fact that she had Room 313 aboard the *Morro Castle.*

*   *   *   *   *

The *Morro Castle* story was the type editors dreamed about, too. It wasn't a one-day story, but had sustained interest over months, even years. Through the disaster inquiry, suits against the steamship line, the trial of First Officer Warms, The Mercury milked the yarn for all it was worth, and the town ate it up!

It took Hill thirty years to approach the thrills of being on the scene of a sea disaster. This was the November 26, 1964, collision of the Norwegian tanker *Stolt Dagali* and the Israeli liner *Shalom,* off the New Jersey coast. It was in the immediate area where the *Morro Castle* was beached, but it wasn't as disastrous, even though 19 lives were lost.

The editor and Mrs. Hill were on one of their annual freighter cruises, a relaxing surcease from jangling telephones, making deadlines and listening to subscribers' complaints.

The couple traveled mostly in the Caribbean on banana boats to Central America, the West Coast and northern South American coasts. They "dangerously" sailed Swedish bauxite ships into the interiors of Surinam and far into Venezuela. They toured the Virgin Islands and Trinidad.

This time they had flown to Los Angeles, then embarked on the *Esparta,* flagship of the United Fruit Line, for a west-to-east cruise. The main objective was another transit of that engineering masterpiece, the Panama Canal.

The *Esparta* was unloading bananas in Los Angeles when

the Pottstown couple had boarded her. Then they had sailed for rainy San Francisco where the remaining banana cargo was discharged. After several days they had left for the South Pacific, with stops scheduled for Nicaragua and Panama, where the ship would be reloaded. Final destination was Weehawken, New Jersey, United's warehouse headquarters.

Thanksgiving was four days off when the *Esparta* traversed the canal. Officers and crew were anxious to be home with their families for the holiday. Discreet suggestions were made to Captain Christian G. Dietz that with fair weather and twenty knots or more sailing, the sailors could make their loved ones happy.

The sailing was smooth, except for usual turbulence off Cape Hatteras, and the ship's pace was steady. The officers, who ate in the same galley with the passengers, were slyly jubilant. It appeared the *Esparta* would dock early on Thanksgiving morning. Then the sailors would have the holiday and Friday to spend at home. They'd sail back on the milk route Saturday.

Captain Dietz was taciturn, but his wife, who accompanied him on voyages, was more voluble. She "leaked" the advice that the *Esparta* would be home early.

The ship arrived at Ambrose Light, in New York harbor, before dawn on Thursday. The pilot came aboard, and now it would be only a few hours until arrival in Weehawken. The day was cold and drizzly. The chill penetrated the warmest overcoat.

Hill was out early on deck, a daily habit, when he noticed unusual activity. The crew was standing by at lifeboats, now dangling off their davits and over the side of the ship. The ship was moving! Yes, it was turning around and heading south in New York harbor!

Hill rushed to the radio operator's room, where he knew he'd find a friendly reception to questions. But the shack was darkened; curtains were pulled over the portholes.

Luckily, Hill saw Mrs. Dietz come out of the captain's

116

quarters. He rushed up the ladder. She met him halfway and exclaimed:

"There's been a collision. We have been ordered to stand by there."

Passengers had access to the wheelhouse, so Hill dashed there. The mate on duty pointed to a blackboard. On it was printed the names *Stolt Dagali* and *Shalom.*

"Those two hit about twenty miles down the bay," he said. "We don't know how bad it is, but we were ordered by the Coast Guard to stand guard and to pick up bodies and survivors."

Hill raced to his cabin to get a radio. Mrs. Hill said,

"There's something on the air about a ship collision."

Hill broke the news to her, and rushed out on deck.

By this time, most of the passengers had heard the news and were on deck. As the ship came into sight of the collision, the passengers saw a huge liner on the starboard. It was the Grace Lines *Santa Rosa,* which had picked up survivors.

On the port side was another mammoth liner. It was the Israeli luxury liner, the *Shalom,* with a gaping hole in her bow.

Directly in front was the forward half of a tanker. The bow stuck out of the ocean like a flagpole. Waves swept over it, and every few seconds someone shouted: "There it goes." They meant it was sinking. They probably got their cues from radio, which was shouting that the *Stolt Dagali* had been struck amidships, cloven in two by the *Shalom,* had sunk and had taken down eleven seamen, including a stewardess.

Yet, there before the *Esparta* was half of the tanker, still floating.

The *Esparta* stopped its engines and went on guard duty. No bodies or survivors were sighted. But the seamen still stood by the lifeboats.

The *Esparta* idled there for several hours. Passengers watched tugs take the stricken *Shalom* in tow. Airplanes swept the skies, seeking survivors. Then Captain Dietz got orders to abandon the search and permission to resume its voyage.

Hill was thinking, as Miss Prince had thought at the *Morro Castle* disaster site: "What a story this will make!" It certainly didn't have the throat tugs of the *Morro Castle* calamity, and the *Esparta's* lives were not in danger.

But Hill took copious notes—and added the real McCoy when the captain's wife said she'd get Hill copies of all the radiograms from the Coast Guard.

The *Esparta* headed back for New York. All passengers missed breakfast, watching the slow tug-pushed *Shalom* make its way to port. The *Esparta* didn't dock at Weehawken until well after noon, and the officers and crew missed half a holiday with their families.

Hill couldn't wait to telephone his eye-witness story to the office. It was used in an eight-column box over the masthead on Page One.

Chapter 17

NOTHING NEW UNDER THE SUN

The war that engulfed almost the entire world had ended with the surrender of Japan. Reader interest had been high for years, but now a return to reporting the prosaic, routine happenings left the reader cold.

Journalism that set The Mercury apart from its contemporaries was absent from Page One. The topics that kept the town buzzing with conversation were missing. Even the local election of 1945 was nothing to write home about. It was a dull period.

Then it cropped up. There was a chance to "make" a story.

Shandy Hill was not adverse to stunts that attracted the reader. He reveled in socking the reader right in the eye with an "astonisher." But he never figured he could go back to the 1890's and early 1900's to titillate his readers.

The day of the "moon hoax" was past. That imaginative piece by R. A. Locke, a New York Sun reporter, got the attention when it gave an account of the inhabitants of the moon. Yet today we are on the threshold of visiting that planet.

As early in newspaperdom as 1874, James Gordon Bennett, Jr., gave his entire Page One of The New York Herald to a sensational account of the escape of wild animals from the zoo. Under headlines reading "A Shocking Sabbath Carnival of Death," the story told of lions and tigers mutilating citizens in "awful combats."

It was wild and woolly, even though the last paragraph said "The entire story given above is a pure fabrication. Not one word of it is true."

Philadelphia newspapers, at the turn of the century, were

119

inclined to revive the "Jersey devil" and "inexplicable happenings in queer places," as a Monday-morning happening after a dull weekend.

This "devil," as revealed in a syndicated story by J. Elfreth Watkins, was said to have been a normal child that "assumed a serpent-like body, with eleven hoofs, the head of a horse, the wings of a bat and the forked tail of a dragon." The weird creature, from the bed of its birth, uttered a series of loud raucous cries, as it flew up a chimney to haunt Jersey's "Big Forest" around Leeds Point, and provide many a newspaper story for dull days.

A hoax may not be news, but its impact may make news. Sightings of unidentified flying objects, dismissed by the United States armed forces as mere misinterpretations of conventional objects, still are sworn to by UFO buffs. This, even though so eminent an authority as Dr. Donald H. Menzel, professor of practical astronomy at Harvard University, reminded the American Society of Newspaper Editors at its 1967 convention that "sightings of flying saucers go far back in history, where they assumed different forms for different people. Old records refer to them as fiery dragons, fiery chariots, wills-o'-the-wisp, jack-o'-lanterns, fire drakes, fox fire and even the devil himself."

*   *   *   *   *

Would the modern-day reader become engrossed in a revival of the "Jersey devil" type of story?

He not only would be, but he would actively participate in a drama that fascinated Pottstown for half a month, frightened the countryside, brought out state police and game protectors, resulted in several shootings, jammed country roads with morbid thrill-seekers' cars, and sent a couple of accident victims to hospitals.

Mass suggestion became so startling that children were locked in their homes and kept from attending school for fear "The Thing" would devour them. A religious woman prayed that the animal might be captured before Sunday, "as otherwise attendance in church and Sunday School will suffer."

Posses, with sometimes as many as a hundred men, all armed with rifles and shotguns, roamed the countryside in search of the "the monster." Bear and wolf traps were baited with fowl and cattle entrails. State police feared trigger-happy hunters would kill off each other, and they stopped automobiles.

The story was reported factually, objectively and without sensationalism by The Mercury. The reports may not have been believed by all, but they were accepted by all as prime subjects for conversation.

Every report of "The Thing" was documented by names and addresses of persons who saw or heard the animal. But the story got out of hand and was hard to turn off. Finally, it was ended, not unlike the "moon hoax," by a tongue-in-cheek statement by a game protector. Yet people today, almost a quarter-century later, swear they saw the weird tanta-lizer.

* * * * *

Jack Binder, an aging staffer with almost fifty years of active reporting, was fascinated by animal tales. He knew accounts of animals and children attract readers. He could spin an engrossing tale from hospital reports when a muskrat bit someone. He bubbled over when police told him a woman in a fashionable part of town saw a mysterious animal with four huge front teeth and a rat-like tail, resembling a small dog. Police investigated, and one officer said he actually held the beast for a time before it escaped his grasp.

Binder came back from police headquarters one early November day with a one-paragraph story about a strange appearing animal roaming the countryside.

Hill glanced at the item and tossed it back.

"Jazz that up a little," he told Binder. "It's dull tonight and we need a story."

121

Binder expanded the yarn to four paragraphs. It was played on Page One, with a small head, at the bottom of a column. It said:

"A strange animal that 'screams like a man' and that is dark in color with a long, rather slender tail, is creating alarm among residents of North Coventry and Cedarville [two Pottstown suburbs].

"That the animal may be a panther or a wildcat escaped from its usual haunts is believed by some residents," the story continued. "They said the animal was living on rabbits, pheasants and other small game. They fear when the small game becomes scarce it may attack farm animals or persons. Half-eaten carcasses of birds and rabbits have been found."

The account quoted two persons as having heard "strange blood-curdling noises. They [the residents] made vain attempts to locate the strange animal."

Then another person, with name and address given, "is said to have seen the animal. It was larger and longer than a fox, different in shape with a tenuous tail."

Miller Long, manager of a show farm near Pottstown, tried to allay fears by announcing the next day that he found "the body of a huge fox" on the farm.

"This ends the career of the so-called 'mystery animal' that was said by some to 'scream like a man,' " The Mercury said, giving the story the same Page-One prominence as the original story.

Not so, said the residents, and the next day the newspaper said, "The finding of the body of a huge gray fox has not ended the terror occasioned by the movements of a strange animal which 'screams like a man,' according to some, and 'cries like a baby' by others."

Binder by now was wrapped in the story.

He provided the name and address of a woman who "was getting her little boy ready for school when she heard an animal 'crying like a baby.' " But the animal, "apparently in a different mood, 'screamed dreadfully' outside the door" of another resident, whose name and address dutifully were given.

Then the hunt was on!

"A posse of six men, armed with shotguns, started on a hunt after farmers said it tried to seize a duck," the story recounted. And "the consensus" was that the animal was a panther!

"Small children traveling on school busses are met at stopping places by parents in cars," the item said.

* * * * *

Not only was "The Thing" heard, but it finally was seen, and The Mercury quoted the viewers with names and addresses.

"An animal with a sleek black coat, a long tenuous tail and short pointed ears, answering the description of a panther, was seen at 6:30 A.M. on the premises of . . ." and the name and address followed.

The witness said he "heard horses in a field snorting and running around in alarm. He saw the mystery animal loping like a huge cat among the horses." Persons across the way "also had a plain view of the animal." One resident "ran out with a rifle, but the animal escaped into the woods."

This situation became so acute on the fourth day of the story that township police announced they'd head a posse to track down the beast. The police chief asked men "to bring shotguns, rifles and 'coon dogs."

Forty men, "armed with high powered rifles," according to the story on the fifth day of the narrative, "turned up for the hunt, but the animal eluded the hunters."

All this time, five more persons heard or saw the animal. "The Thing" visited a turkey farm, but when lights were turned on in the pens, the beast bounded away "like a great cat." A small-game hunter, crossing a field high with weeds and underbush, "suddenly saw a sleek black animal leap twenty feet high in front of him and then dash away." This witness said he "fired at it, but missed."

The screams of the beast were "blood-curdling" to a local woman, and the police said another posse of at least a hundred men would start out the next morning to track the animal. The policemen said " 'Coon dogs are not good on this hunt because we can't give them the scent of the animal."

*   *   *   *   *

These hundred were hampered by ugly weather, and they found nothing. But Peter J. Filkosky, state game protector in Montgomery County, joined the search. He conferred with persons who heard of or saw "The Thing." He reported he didn't think the panther theory held water, but he couldn't account for the howls. The game expert said fifty years had passed since a black panther roamed this area, but admitted one might have escaped from a circus menagerie or zoo.

"I think there's more danger from stray rifle shots and shotgun pellets than from the animal itself," Filkosky warned. He just had received the first complete description of the animal, right down to inches. One who saw it said "the animal was 38 inches long, 18 inches in height, with short ears and a jet-black body. The size of the body is like that of a small collie dog," the describer continued. "The hair is smooth and shiny." The head was described as being "somewhat like a show dog."

Witnesses disagreed. A woman motorist said she saw a puma on a road. It passed in front of her car, and "seemed in no particular hurry." She said she recognized it for its color, its fine head, long body and long tail." She said two pumas escaped from a nearby circus, and may be roaming the local area. The Mercury prominently displayed the picture of a puma with the story.

The same day's account said, "The search for 'The Thing' was featured by the use of 15 fox hounds supplied by a member of a local hunting club. The baying of the hounds could be heard for miles around."

The only bag was a gray fox.

Police reported finding prints made by an animal's paws, and preserved them for experts' study. Two hunters saw "The Thing" at night, fired at it, but it "gave a shrill cry and disappeared with leaps of ten feet or more in length."

By the ninth day of the hunt, the story commanded top position. It was reported in a page-wide Page-One box over the flag. The Mercury said: "Casualties mount to four as the mystery animal continues to evade posses." An eighteen-year-old boy shot himself in the left thigh when he tripped over a log and his gun fired. A girl was shot in the arm in a similar accident. Two persons were injured when their autos collided in the hunt. A woman homeowner complained she was tired of the number of persons parking their autos and tramping over her property at night.

"Maybe I'll start some shooting if this nonsense doesn't stop," she warned.

Her complaint may have been justified. "Bumper to bumper motorcars clogged the roads," the paper reported. Cars from points as far as 25 miles away joined the carnival. Fifteen state policemen augmented the search, "but the terror successfully evaded them," the paper said, "as well as 12 game protector deputies."

And the heat went on. Police decided to set beartraps. They scattered cattle entrails and fresh blood in the woods to attract the beast. More residents saw the animal. One hunter had a wild experience. He related he "saw two huge yellow eyes gleaming from an oak tree in the beam of the flashlight. He was getting ready to shoot when all of a sudden a huge screech owl took to its wings. It had a wingspread of six feet. The hunter was so surprised he didn't fire his gun."

* * * * *

Fear was heightened. Supply men stopped deliveries in the neighborhood, the newspaper said—at least until the panther is caught, a paid advertisement proclaimed. This had its recompenses. A paragraph said: "Housewives are pleased to see canvassers and collectors at their doors decreased."

Hill, in a light daily editorial page column he wrote under the title, "All Around the Town," reported, "The mournful meanderings of the mystery terror have caused many reminiscences of similar scares. One of the oddest was the odyssey of the 'Wild Man of Chestnut Hill.' [A section near Pottstown]: The wild man who frightened women and children turned out to be a hermit who lived in a shack in the Chestnut Hill vastness. He grew a long beard and presented horrific appearances. But he didn't harm anybody. Sympathetic neighbors placed the alleged eccentric in an almshouse.

"Five years ago residents of Pruss Hill began to hear eerie sounds and they envisioned a wild animal in their midst. One resident said he saw a mountain lion leap over the hood of his automobile when he was traveling a lonely road. Next came a motorist with an 'imprint' of a lion's paw on his auto hood. Both reports proved hoaxes.

"Chester County, adjacent to Montgomery County, had other crises. Several years ago a mischievous prankster frightened the countryside by donning an animal skin and darting in front of motorists when dusk was descending. It took a while to capture him, but the feat was accomplished.

"Elected officials in the area were made the butt of practical jokes. One official received through the mail a package of salt. The sender suggested he put it on the animal's tail to capture it. Another official received a telephone call telling him the 'terror' was on his front porch. It was a small rabbit."

* * * * *

The curious jammed the roads as the search went on. State police were ordered to patrol the hills all night long, especially to search cars for loaded rifles. They reiterated this was illegal.

Deputy game commissioners set a dozen wolf traps. Each deputy carried a high powered rifle and revolver, ready to shoot.

126

But the story was losing its steam, even though wire services clamored for daily stories. Pottstown was gaining notoriety, The Mercury said, through widespread publicity throughout the United States.

There was a shortage of new angles, but the newspaper's awesome responsibility to maintain order became overwhelming. Finally, Hill told the editorial department to kill the yarn before someone got killed. Police, state and local, agreed.

After sixteen days of squeezing every ounce of sustenance from the story, Hill decided on a two-column Page-One box, ascribed to Game Protector Filkosky. This box, under a head—"Game Protector Declares 'Terror' Has Moved Away; Far, Far Away—said:

"Yesterday Game Warden Peter J. Filkosky closed the incident with the report: 'Over the weekend I was visited by Barefoot Charley, a sourdough from Alaska. Barefoot Charley reported that when he was driving down to Pennsylvania, he saw the 'terror' pass him on the Alcan Highway. The 'terror' was running at a speed of 40 miles an hour and going in the opposite direction."

Chapter 18

SAVING AN INDUSTRY

Changing the entire physical complexion of the community, modernizing its laws, possibly changing its thinking, were accomplishments ascribed to Shandy Hill. Yet he brushed off lightly any encomiums. The crusades were just part of his job, he said.

Even the incredible honor of having fought and won forty-one reform campaigns in two years, as a staffer figured out, rested lightly on his shoulders.

But the one achievement he most treasured was saving an industry and 1,400 jobs for Pottstown. He didn't do this alone. He had help. But the denouement came after he stuck out his neck to risk his health as an intermediary in a strike.

World War II veterans came back home in 1945 to find they no longer had their jobs at the Spicer Manufacturing Corporation plant. Seniority no longer was considered, so, when workers of low seniority were put to work, the United Auto Workers walked out.

This, at least, was given by The Mercury as a reason for a two-month strike that climaxed a long series of running battles between union and management.

The final of three early-1945 strikes came in the spring, just about the time the war in Europe was ending, and management decided to close the plant for all time. It wasn't a hollow threat, even though such gestures had been made before on the restless union, without effect.

This final decision came in the home of John B. Bohannon, plant manager. It was made by Charles S. Dana, sturdy industrialist who was 87 in 1968 and still chairman of the company which now bears his name—The Dana Corporation, with plants in Pennsylvania, Ohio and Indiana.

Dismayed by the workers' unrest and strikes, Dana glowered at Lloyd Haney, labor relations director of the Dana empire. Shandy Hill was the fourth person in Bohannon's living room, where the labor situation was being discussed.

"Sit down at that typewriter," Dana ordered Haney, "and write a full-page advertisement for The Mercury saying we are going to close shop for all time. If we can't get the plant back to work, we'll shut it."

The three bystanders protested. Haney, Bohannon and then Hill each tried to dissuade Dana from going through with his rash resolution.

*   *   *   *   *

Dana was a New York lawyer who had left the Bar to become administrative head of the Spicer Universal Joint Manufacturing Company thirty years before.

A graduate of Columbia University Law School, who had earned a master's degree in international law in 1904 at the age of 23, he had thought of making a career in the U.S. Department of State, but gave up the idea in favor of the law. He had served on the staff of the Pennyslvania Railroad's legal counsel and the staffs of two New York district attorneys.

While serving under District Attorney William Travers Jerome, he had assisted in the prosecution of Henry K. Thaw for the murder of Stanford White, one of the most spectacular cases in American history.

In 1914, Dana bought a controlling interest in the Spicer company, after Clarence Spicer told him he needed refinancing for his Plainfield, N.J., plant or would have to close the up-and-coming company. Dana combined his administrative talents with Spicer's inventive genius to make Spicer—which manufactured universal joints—one of the leading contributors to the growth of automobile transportation.

Spicer located in Pottstown in the fall of 1919. It occupied buildings in which the Chadwick six-cylinder automobile—an early-American car built shortly after the turn of the century—had been manufactured. Spicer started production in Pottstown in February, 1920. In 1946, the organization's name was changed to Dana Corporation.

Spicer's thrived in Pottstown for many years under a "company" union. This independent union had a rather informal three-page agreement with the company. But in 1943, the Pottstown union joined the United Auto Workers. A more binding agreement was sought, leading to many disagreements between management and union.

On the last day of July, 1944, the United Auto Workers asked the United States Government (the industrial plants were under governmental supervision) to take over the plant and remove Bohannon. A second appeal went to President Franklin D. Roosevelt. The UAW urged the War Labor Board and President Roosevelt to seize the plant in order to assure peak war production, "which is being sabotaged by management."

At that time, workers walked out of the plant. Harper Diener, president of the fledgling local, said the strike was unauthorized. Bohannon declared that the strike was sponsored by union officials.

The differences were compromised, and the workers resumed their places in the shop after four days. But this strike was a forerunner of long and serious labor-management trouble.

Management and company were attempting diligently to negotiate a contract during twenty months of dickering. Bohannon, who was friendly with Hill, asked The Mercury newsman to sit in on some of the negotiations as a stabilizing influence. Hill agreed. He got as far as the negotiating table, but the union objected and sent him packing.

Negotiations reached another impasse, and a walkout took place from April 24 to May 7, 1945. It was said to have stemmed from the union's dissatisfaction with a War Labor

Board decision on terms and conditions of employment at the plant handed down April 21, 1945, after months of hearings.

A lengthy brief touched on many points of contention, setting an eight-hour day and a 40-hour week, starting pay of 55 cents an hour for production jobs and 65 cents an hour for nonproduction (with no discrimination in rates of pay because of sex), and a seniority clause that was to provoke further contention, because management and union had separate ideas of how it was to be applied.

The seniority clause said: "Seniority shall be by departments except in case of layoffs, extending over a period of more than thirty days. Seniority shall be by hiring date by the company, and employees shall be offered re-employment in line with their seniority on the jobs they are capable of doing."

The National Labor Relations Board threw out a request for the same wage scale paid by the Dana Corporation at its plant in Toledo, Ohio.

So the workers walked out for another two weeks, even though the War Labor Board said the work stoppage was illegal. As the end of the war in Europe approached, the company saw loss of contracts, and the union seethed. The clash hardly was softened by a company announcement that Spicer planned to lay off 1,400 workers because of the loss of war contracts. Bohannon said, "Hardly more than 500 will be employed." He closed the plant on August 20, 1945, pending rescheduling of work and reemployment.

The union balked at the way workers were being recalled. The UAW insisted layoffs and recalls had to be made according to seniority and with no pay cut. The union asserted its contract with the company called for accrued seniority for veterans with low seniority, the union walked out once more, on the first day of peace-time work.

Recognizing the seriousness of this strike, Hill asked to meet with the union's bargaining committee. He promised to print in The Mercury any union statement "word for word, comma for comma, period for period," as long as it wasn't libelous.

Sam Shervone, stocky, cigar-chomping, loud UAW international representative, said he'd write such a statement, but he put it off. Instead, at a union mass meeting, he denounced The Mercury. The paper answered him editorially and backed its promise with corroboration by the union secretary that The Mercury indeed had promised to publish a union statement without blue-penciling it.

Shervone was on the spot. He wrote the union's side of the strike, and The Mercury published it word for word, comma for comma, and period for period. Hill thought Shervone at least would say "thank you" after The Mercury kept its word, but no statement came from the labor leader.

Hill telephoned him and asked: "How'd you like the treatment of the story?"

Answered Shervone, "I didn't think you'd do it."

* * * * *

As the idleness of Spicer's grew into weeks, Dana came to Pottstown. He asked Haney to fly in from Toledo.

"Sit down and write an advertisement," he told Haney in Bohannon's Pottstown home. "That will get the plant to work. If it doesn't do it, we will have to close shop."

Dana had won national recognition for his straightforward method of settling a strike that was paralyzing automotive plants in Toledo during the Depression. He was quoted as having said at the end of the strike: "I felt it was a privilege to work to provide jobs for you. There is only one thing really worthwhile about an organization; and that is its men and women. Stone and mortar, bricks and machinery can be duplicated, but the workers cannot."

In 1945 he didn't meet with the union, or if he did, his meeting was not publicized. So Haney, Bohannon and Hill argued with him that he couldn't close the plant.

The talk went on loudly for hours. Finally the three drafted an innocuous advertisement that met with Dana's approval. It said only two issues remained unresolved—the practicability of plantwide seniority and the question of the pay rate. A plea was made that the workers return to work while negotiations continued.

The advertisement produced results. But Bohannon, manager of the plant for fifteen years, lost his job. He asked Dana to accept his resignation, "which has been on your desk for several weeks." The union voted on October 11 to go back to work after a two-month layoff.

Hill went to a sickbed with nervous exhaustion.

Chapter 19

WHO'S MORE COMPLACENT?

Early in 1945, Secretary of State John Foster Dulles erected verbal "no-trespassing" signs to Russians on more than one-quarter of United States soil.

He declared 27 percent of the U.S. off limits to Russians, in reprisal against similar curbs against Americans in the Soviet Union. The new role applied to all Soviet citizens in the country, except approximately 50 accredited to the United Nations as employees of the United Nations Secretariat.

Pottstown was within the proscribed area.

The Mercury recognized that this was merely a harmless skirmish in the Cold War. So Shandy Hill whimsically asked editorially: "Can you picture a crew of Russian agents defying arrest, combing the streets of Pottstown for whatever is so vital here that Washington had to label the community 'verboten' to them?

"The flaw in the whole picture," continued The Mercury, "is that effective Communist agents do not go around wearing beards or using thick Russian accents or other identifying marks."

It might make good cartoon captions to put Moscow, Idaho, off limits, and good security to guard closely the Mexican and Canadian borders, but certainly no Russian agent would come to Pottstown! Or, if he did, he certainly would not go unnoticed long, or would he?

The question was batted around for a while at an editorial conference. After some mental gymnastics, Hill asked, "Just what would happen if we'd put a uniformed Russian on the street? How long would he go undetected before one of our patriotic citizens flattened him? Would anybody care?"

The thought was intriguing. It gripped the editorial staff, especially Normand R. Poirier, a lucid feature writer, so he was assigned to do the story.

But where to get a Russian uniform? Theatrical costume equippers in Philadelphia were combed without success. A Media, Pennsylvania, firm had such material, The Mercury was told. But the advice was wrong. Then an Allentown costumer was said to have a Russian Army uniform, but a trip there disclosed the uniform was of World War I vintage.

About this time, Life magazine pictured on its cover a young Russian soldier eyeing two pretty girls. He was dressed immaculately with sort of a Sam Brown belt and high boots. "There's our model," Hill cried.

The Mercury enlisted a New York friend to canvass theatrical costumers there. Finally, an East Side firm came up with a modern Russian officer's uniform, but there would be a slight delay because an epaulette had been torn off, and it needed other alterations.

The Mercury fretted about the loss of time. Almost three weeks passed from the time the story idea germinated until the uniform was mailed to Pottstown.

* * * * *

Poirier made a perfect foil for the job. He was tall, slender, erect. The field-green uniform was complemented with a heavy gray brass-buttoned overcoat. Red and gold epaulettes were on the shoulders, and a gray hat had a hammer and sickle and a red star above its visor. Heavy, high black boots completed the outfit.

A local amateur actress painted a thin black mustache on Poirier's upper lip, and the Russian colonel was ready to go to work.

The Mercury staffer was put on a train several miles outside Pottstown, with orders to speak no English, but to tour the town until "discovered." The Mercury provided a strong-arm guard to shadow the "colonel."

135

The "colonel" found the State Department's "Iron Curtain" was made of chintz. Colorfully garbed and as prominent as a bandaged finger in a symphony orchestra, he roamed Pottstown at will. He rode the train, snapped pictures of forbidden plants, dropped "poison pills" into the water supply, "blew up" a bridge and mingled with the "peasants."

The "colonel" drank in bars, shopped in markets, bought stamps at the Post Office, purchased vodka in a state liquor store and caviar at a supermarket and passed three local policemen, snapping pictures with a camara he carried quite openly.

For more than four hours, no one seriously challenged him—not even police—until after his stint was ended.

Some surprised eyebrows were lifted, and one news tipster rushed into The Mercury breathlessly to tell the editor he saw a "Russian spy and an accomplice shadowing him." But no report was made to police, or by police.

Poirier wrote, "It was an unnerving experience, sometimes frightening, sometimes maddening." He confessed in his stories that he reasonably expected to be shot in the back. But he went unharmed physically until a "reenactment" for television a few days later.

His lark was most ludicrous when he went into a mainstem bistro and ordered, in a thick guttural voice: "Vodka!"

The bartender couldn't understand him, so the colonel finally asked for gin, pronouncing it "jean." He tossed off several drinks while an obfuscated patron shouted, "Hey, buddy, what outfit you in?" Poirier didn't reply, so a group argued the point. One customer was sure the uniformed visitor was a high-ranking Salvation Army officer.

The Mercury staffer, in all his purchases, pretended he didn't know American money. He laid down bills and coins, depending on the clerk to make change. All were honest, but none asked questions about his unawareness of the value of money.

The "colonel" was walking back to the newspaper late in

the afternoon when he heard a male voice behind him call: "Hey, mister!" It was repeated, "Hey, mister!"

Poirier tried to ignore it, feigning unfamiliarity with the English language. On a third "Hey, mister!" he turned. It was a Pottstown plainclothes detective. After recognition, the policeman excused himself with, "I knew you all the time."

* * * * *

The Associated Press sent pictures of the "colonel's" adventure around the world. Editor and Publisher, the newspaper trade journal, telephoned New York, saying it would hold its weekly edition pending arrival of pictures. The NBC, CBS and ABC radio-TV networks all used pictures and stories.

The Columbia Broadcasting System asked whether The Mercury staffer would reenact the story for Eric Sevareid's Sunday television feature, "The American Week." The Mercury agreed; it would be a good national promotion.

Overwhelmed by the national acceptance of this story, The Mercury editorialized, "It was not a 'stunt' designed to amuse folks. It was developed after careful thought to bring Pottstown's attention to our growing apathy, the average person's 'don't care' attitude, his 'it-can't-happen-here' stance. Let's be on our toes."

* * * * *

There was a slight hitch when CBS said it would come in Friday to do the story all over again. The Russian colonel's uniform had gone back to the New York costumer. But CBS said it would bring it back. This entailed going through thousands of packages in the New York Post Office before the clothing was found.

A television crew of four, including a director, worked for four hours, shooting 1,500 feet of film while The Mercury staffer retraced his steps.

The climactic scene was staged at Pottstown's busiest

downtown intersection. Poirier was going through his paces, cameras grinding.

Suddenly, three shopworkers, in town to cash their paychecks, burst out of a saloon.

"You dirty communist!" they yelled. "We'll run you out of town!"

They grappled with Poirier, and tried to push him into an automobile. They ripped off a shoulderboard, punched him in the face and scratched his cheek.

Two uniformed Pottstown policemen stood by, enjoying what they thought was part of the scenario. When Poirier was wrestled to the ground, they stepped in to stop the fracas.

The Mercury headlined the story: "Red Colonel TV Film Disturbed by Scuffle."

* * * * *

The sad part of it all was that CBS didn't use the story on Eric Sevareid's program that Sunday afternoon. A CBS spokesman said the film was tops, but "it couldn't be dovetailed into the solemn report that was made on the tense Formosan situation."

At that time, Chiang Kai-shek slowly was being pushed out of the mainland and into his island fortress, and the Russian colonel was edged, indeed, into television limbo.

Chapter 20

ENFORCING THE LAW

Sometimes the inaction—or the behind-the-scenes hidden action—of the Pottstown Police Department was ludicrous. The Mercury capitalized on this, for the "leaks" in the department were large enough to drive a four-horse team through. Patrolmen kept no secrets from The Mercury—and the newspaper satirized the leaks with telling effect.

Police executives' attempts to hide the news reacted against the department, and hastened the day when favoritism would be barred and the law enforced without partiality.

In the great VIP (Very Important People) case that convulsed Pottstown for a week, The Mercury's treatment inflated a minor disorderly conduct charge, which ordinarily might have been used as a single paragraph, into a farce that finally forced the municipality's chief executive into arresting one of his closest friends.

Had there been honesty in docketing the case, it might even have been overlooked, but because no record was made of arrests, The Mercury had a chance to headline the department's dishonesty. The newspaper was carrying out one of its duties to examine everything that appeared faulty.

The Mercury headlined on a Tuesday morning: "A Pottstown industrialist and his business associate were 'pinched' early Saturday morning after a run-in with two patrolmen. But they were 'sprung' within hours after the wheels of brass started whirling in one of the most blatant coverups attempted in local police circles."

The news account chronicled how two "rookie" policemen, Dan Kegel and Jack Paretti, arrested two alleged disorderly motorists on the main street. The police advised less noise, but the two revelers reportedly swore, then one rudely pushed a patrolman. The two were taken to the jail and placed in a cell.

According to The Mercury's informant, Desk Sergeant John Kirlin recognized the two suspects. He allegedly telephoned his immediate superior, Sergeant Irvin K. Frederick, and because "dynamite" was recognized in the arrest, Sergeant Frederick was said to have rushed to the home of Mayor John B. Hartenstine, Jr., bosom pal of one of the men in the jailhouse.

Hartenstine, aroused from a deep slumber, came down into his kitchen to tell the police sergeant:

"Because we're friends and they're reputable citizens, they won't run away. There is no sense in keeping them in jail."

The jailed were "sprung."

No report of the pickup appeared anywhere in the police station. Hartenstine and Chief of Police James A. Laughead denied knowing anything about the incident.

*   *   *   *   *

So who were the VIPs? The Mercury asked this the following day.

The paper printed some pictures of the town's foremost industrialists and business leaders, then answered the question: "No, these are not the VIP's picked up early Saturday morning."

What did VIP mean? The Mercury guessed it might be "Void If Plastered" or "Valuable Inside Pals."

The next day the chairman of the police civil service commission succinctly, if inelegantly, said, "The deal stinks."

As all Pottstown giggled and guessed (many surmised correctly) who the VIPs were, The Mercury went into great detail how the pressure to drop the charges was reached in Mayor Hartenstine's home.

So complete were the details that by Saturday, the mayor decided to undo the "fix." Accompanied by William J. Boden, Sr., Republican political leader, Hartenstine came to

140

The Mercury to ask for a conference with Hill.

"What do you want me to do?" asked Hartenstine.

"Enforce the law," replied The Mercury editor.

Hartenstine not only ordered warrants sworn out against his two friends, but he volunteered a public apology.

"I owe an apology to all the people of Pottstown," he declared. And these words were inscribed in The Mercury for history. "What I did was detrimental to the police department."

The two young policemen brought charges against the mayor's two friends. Each was released on $20 bail. Neither appeared for a hearing, and their bail was forfeited to the borough.

The story was ended.

* * * * *

This byplay was in contrast to the way at least one Pottstonian reacted to Shandy Hill's off-repeated admonition to his friends: "Get yourself caught in a love nest, and the story goes right on Page One: This goes for everybody."

Hill insisted "crime news" about himself be printed right on Page One, too. He deserved the same treatment, he said, when he ran afoul of the law. So, when he was ticketed for jaywalking (a law his own Mercury proposed) the story was published on Page One. Also when he was cited for speeding one Easter Sunday morning shortly after he attended church, the story got the usual treatment.

This policy always was a challenge to those who came into the editorial room to plead, "Please keep my arrest out of the paper," or "Don't use my son's name," even if he did steal a car or burglarize a home. Without fear or favor, that news went into the paper.

* * * * *

A pillar of the community once asked that news of his errant brother be kept out of the paper. Hill suggested: "I'll tell you what we'll do. You keep your brother out of jail, and we'll keep him out of the paper."

141

One lazy Sunday afternoon, Hill was relaxing over the papers when his telephone rang.

On the other end was Ernst Struckmann, general manager of the nationally known Mrs. Smith's Pie Company.

"I knew you would find this out, and I want to be the first to tell you," Struckmann said.

"You always said your friends get the same treatment in The Mercury as your detractors. Well, I want you to know I was in a long, hard bargaining session with the bakers' union in Philadelphia. I got a little boisterous when stopped by police on the way back to Pottstown Sunday morning and I was pinched and tossed into the jug. Just so you know, Shandy. I knew you'd want this."

Struckmann was thanked. His arrest in a small suburb of Philadelphia might have gone unreported. But his story appeared on Page One of The Mercury that Monday morning.

*   *   *   *   *

This impartial treatment of the news did not mean the newspaper could not bend over backwards with a charitable attitude—especially if some innocent person might be hurt. Hill never took much time to listen to the stereotyped, oft-repeated and untrue plea of the transgressors who asked: "Please don't print that I was arrested. It will kill my mother, who has a heart disease." If all the mothers allegedly so affected had died after publication of the news, the cemeteries would have been filled!

The Mercury had an odd policy on suicides that some other editors could not understand. First of all, The Mercury never used attempted suicides. Those poor persons who found life so unbearable that they attempted to take their lives often recovered and regained a constructive outlook toward life. So why have the finger of scorn pointed at them?

When a person ended his own life, the newspaper gave the cause. No shillyshallying. The Mercury said the coroner issued a certificate of death by suicide.

But there was one more charitable policy. The Mercury never published the list of his survivors. Not his widow nor his children. The reason: Why should the innocent suffer from the foolhardy stunt of a person who must have been bereft of his senses?

Likewise, The Mercury took cognizance of the pregnant women who weren't able to snare the father until a few days or few months before the wedding ceremony. Everyone knows the first baby can come any time, but . . . .

Sometimes unusual aspects resulted from this sort of protection, especially from wedding anniversaries, which The Mercury printed. A businessman called Hill and said: "Please don't use our 25th wedding anniversary on Friday. You see, our son is that old and he'll know."

Request granted!

* * * * *

He never knew it, but the Rev. Dr. Gustav W. Weber, a Lutheran minister who now is president of Susquehanna University in Selinsgrove, Pennsylvania, drew many laughs in the editorial department when he breathlessly rushed there early one evening.

Dr. Weber was raising some funds for his parish by staging a professional carnival on a lot near his church.

"You know about it," he said, "because one of your reporters was down on the lot. But I swear I didn't know it was there."

When he calmed down, he said the carnival people, without his permission, rang in a "hootchy-kootchy" show of wriggling, dancing girls. And what would his congregation say?

Not only didn't The Mercury know about this show, but it would have had no reason to "cover" it. So it was easy to comply with Dr. Weber's request.

* * * * *

It was a long struggle, but a successful one, in the matter

143

of education, but the community caught on. The Mercury believes it was one of the first small-town newspapers to rid its columns of such vague crime charges as "misdemeanors" or "morals charges." The paper felt it got more people wondering about misdemeanors and morals charges than if it came right out and used the specific words—rape, adultery, sodomy, incest. So it did.

This policy was initiated more than 35 years ago before sex was a drawing-room conversation subject. Pottstown was a small, clannish town, where tongues wag incessantly and the editor was known to all. The first time The Mercury used the word "syphilis" the community was shocked, probably because of past criticism of so-called sensationalism in the newspapers.

But the town got over the shock, mainly because of The Mercury's emphasis that it was dedicated to printing all the news with candor. Certainly it subscribed to a cardinal rule of journalism that the newspaper should be clean, that it should avoid the suggestive or salacious. The newspaper never planned to offend good taste or lower the moral tone of its readers.

*   *   *   *   *

Still a taboo on many newspapers is the use of juveniles' names in crime stories. Some courts and police departments do not make public those names. The Mercury had no trouble with the police or courts, suggesting: You make available all the news, and the newspaper will decide what to use—and be responsible for such publication.

It worked.

For more than thirty years, The Mercury has been using juveniles' names in crime stories, convinced that the searchlight of publicity deters crime. The newspaper believes this worked well, because the youths knew if they stole a car or were arrested for underage drinking, their names would appear in print, probably on Page One. Many thought a second time before committing a crime, police told the paper.

When the paper put this policy into effect, it was shocking to the community. It was shocking to parents—especially those of the "better" class, whatever that is. It was all right to use the names of teen-age offenders when they came from across the tracks, they reasoned. But the "better" class? Horrors!

"Aggrieved" parents claimed The Mercury was not charitable. The Mercury was charitable to persons in difficulty, especially young persons. But in the enforcement of the law, it was society against the trespasser. The community and not the newspaper was the aggrieved party. Parents of other boys and girls had a right to know which of their children's friends were breaking the laws.

The good names of innocent children have a right to protection. And The Mercury published a great deal more news about the "good" children of the community, despite the hue and cry of a few "aggrieved" parents who charge sensationalism. The one outstanding argument The Mercury used with those persons was the people's right to know. That right belonged to the paper's readers, and it could not be suspended.

Chapter 21

THEY'RE WELCOMED HOME

There is no substitute for ideas in publishing an attractive newspaper—and the successful culmination of brilliant ideas is what made The Mercury so well known coast to coast.

The Mercury was popular and respected at home because it had so much reader participation. Its fund-raising campaigns were so numerous and so uniformly successful that the newspaper couldn't help but appeal to all strata of society. Everybody got in the act!

A little luck might have been an ingredient in this success, but usually it was enterprise, hard work, well-laid plans and cooperation from high sources that developed the idea—sometimes coarsely called a "stunt." Enterprise becomes apparent when newspapermen feel themselves part of something nobly worthwhile. Possibly that is why The Mercury's readers and staff writers entered into promotions so wholeheartedly.

There was the prisoner of war caper of 1953 that had papers all over the United States using a Mercury photo on Page One. It was of a little girl rushing up an airplane ramp to embrace her Air Force father just released from a North Korean prisoner-of-war camp.

Correspondents said they shed tears when they saw this photo.

*   *   *   *   *

Shandy Hill had advance word that Pottstown servicemen liberated from Korean prisoner-of-war camps soon would be returned to San Francisco. "Why not send these men's families to San Francisco to greet them?" he reasoned. "And without letting the servicemen know—as a big surprise?"

It could be a heartwarming "stunt." Readers were asked to

146

make contributions to defer expense of the trip. Within a few days, subscribers had sent in $1,600, sufficient to fly the Pottstown folks to San Francisco and back!

The prisoners were Captain Joseph O'Conner of the Air Force and Lt. Frank Kuzmech of the Infantry. They were among some of the 3,597 Americans repatriated, beginning August 6, 1953. Both were flown to Tokyo on September 7 for hospitalization. From there, they were to come to the United States.

*   *   *   *   *

Captain O'Conner was married, the father of two children, Lee Ann, seven, and Patrick Michael, three. The Mercury decided to fly Mrs. O'Conner and the two children to the Coast. The captain's mother, Mrs. Thomas L. O'Conner, was to go along at her own expense.

Lieutenant Kuzmech was unmarried. His parents, Mr. and Mrs. John Kuzmech, were to be the benefactors of Pottstown's generosity.

Suddenly, little time remained for arrangements, because John Murphy, the San Francisco public information officer, alerted Hill, an old college acquaintance, that Captain O'Conner would arrive by airplane at Travis Air Force Base, north of San Francisco, in two days. Lieutenant Kuzmech was coming home by troopship.

That presented problems, but details worked out nicely. Hurriedly, airplane reservations were made, and the two families left by automobile for New York at 4 in the morning, with a Mercury staffer and photographer.

Captain O'Conner arrived at Travis Air Force Base on September 18. Kuzmech was to arrive two days later by ship, so the O'Conners had a pleasant reunion in a San Francisco hotel for several days.

Kuzmech was the most astonished when he saw his parents at dockside. He had written them not to come to San Francisco because he knew they didn't have the money.

Daily stories, telephoned from San Francisco, kept Mercury readers and especially the contributors, advised of the homecoming celebration. The Associated Press, through National Picture Editor Al Resch, offered the use of wire facilities for picture transmission to Philadelphia, where The Mercury picked up the pictures by messenger.

Little Lee Ann O'Conner provided the best and most widely used photograph. She rushed up the gangplank, arms outstretched, to embrace her daddy. Tall, thin Captain O'Conner, bent almost in half to descend to her height, also had his arms ready for a hug. The Mercury photographer caught them in this tableau. When Editor Resch saw the shot, he ordered it on all Associated Press wires.

*   *   *   *   *

Shandy Hill had a compulsion "to do something for the soldiers"—in World War II, in the Korean conflict, and again in the Vietnam war. He wrote them personal letters, asking parents and relatives to send in their addresses. He published their replies, but withheld personal references. Sure, it was "smalltown," but effective journalism.

He urged readers, and especially clubs, to send them Christmas packages. He supervised shipping those packages to army and fleet post offices. When the Salvation Army joined in the Christmas package shipment, he made sure a copy of The Mercury went into every bundle.

This led to a "Bundles-for-Buddies" campaign when servicemen were sent overseas in the Vietnam war. He asked for funds to airmail the papers to army and fleet post offices for every overseas serviceman. The Mercury bundled a week's supply, and every Marine, soldier and sailor in the Pottstown area got a bundle a week. Readers gladly furnished the money for mailing. This fund is operating to this day.

*   *   *   *   *

The heartbreak that some soldiers might have suffered 3,000 miles away from home on a Thanksgiving Day led to an idea that warmed the entire community of Pottstown in 1940.

148

The National Guard had just been called up, and citizen soldiers from Oregon and Washington were bivouacked at a staging area of Indiantown Gap, 80 miles from Pottstown. They were preparing for overseas duty.

A few weeks before Thanksgiving, Hill telephoned the commanding officer at Indiantown Gap to see whether he thought the soldiers would like to come to Pottstown for Thanksgiving Day.

Hill's plan was to farm out these soldiers, one to a Pottstown family. It would have to be potluck. Some would get sumptious feasts, others less pretentious. But they would be with "folks"!

The Mercury asked Pottstown families to adopt a soldier for a day, suggesting dinner, possibly an auto tour of nearby historic Valley Forge, or just a drowsy day at home. It would break up military routine.

The response was terrific. Hundreds of families responded, and Indiantown Gap was told almost daily: "We need more volunteers. Get more men!"

Then the program was enlarged. Pottstown families were asked to have their dinners around noon or early afternoon because the visiting soldiers and their hosts were to be guests at a public reception that night. There would be gifts of candy and cigarettes for every soldier, dance music by a volunteer orchestra, a buffet supper at 11 and refreshments.

Early on Thanksgiving morning, the soldiers left Indiantown Gap by truck. A police escort met them on a highway outside Pottstown and they were brought to The Mercury.

Truck after truck rolled into town, the soldiers lined up on the sidewalks while the host families waited across the street. A captain in charge called the roll, and as each man was called, he stepped forward to be greeted by a family. They whisked him off to their home.

Sadly, there were not enough soldiers to go around. Many Pottstown families were disappointed.

Curfew time was midnight, and their departure was as throat-tightening as if they'd been local boys. Hugs and

149

kisses, long requests, "Be sure to write," and some reluctance to return to camp rewarded Pottstown for its hospitality.

*　　*　　*　　*　　*

This may illustrate what a small-town newspaper can do in the way of public service. There are many other ways.

"What can we do for you?" Hill asked Indiantown Gap the next day when he checked with Army officials as to how the party went.

"We need coat hangers," said the officer. "There's a shortage of wire hangers here."

There was a shortage of metal everywhere, but The Mercury asked Pottstown residents to bring hangers downtown on Saturday. The Mercury knew plenty were around, but it didn't figure Pottstown would swamp the business section! Firemen strung lines from light standard to light standard. The people were asked to place the hangers on the ropes.

The response was so heavy the light standards buckled.

This interest in and concern for the man in the armed services was recognized in 1965 by the Department of Pennsylvania, Jewish War Veterans of the United States of America. In a state convention, the Jewish War Veterans made Shandy Hill "the man of the year."

Chapter 22

MYSTERY NEVER DISCLOSED

A favorite eating spot for newsmen and printers was Harry Lebo's seafood house. A light snack of say, clam stew, was ideal for a deskman at 10:30 P.M. lunchtime. It packed lots of energy, but wasn't too heavy.

Shandy Hill sipped the buttery smoothness of the stew and chewed the clams one night. They were often tough, those clams, but not so chewy as that batch. He chewed and chewed, and then decided something was wrong. He spat out a piece of chewing gum!

Hill was irate, and made more so by the needling of his tablemates. He called the proprietor and proceeded to chew out the cook in several hundred ill-chosen words. The owner listened attentively, waiting until the torrent of words no longer engulfed him. Then he sadly shook his head and mused:

"I wonder how it got in there."

*　　*　　*　　*　　*

The phlegmatic reaction was enough to render anyone speechless. The guffaws of Hill's newspaper-mates didn't help any, either.

It may be inelegant to repeat this experience, but Hill often wondered "how that got in there" when he personally conducted a probe that won for him first honors in a Pennsylvania Society of Newspaper Editors investigative reporting competition. For the parties involved—Pottstown municipal officials and the U.S. Veterans Administration— never could explain how what looked like a bit of secret dealing "got in there" on a United States document.

The secret agreement cost Pottstown homeowners large

amounts of money in assessments for street paving, although the government document codicil guaranteed that the "borough will do the street paving at its own expense and shall levy no assessment upon the developer or the ultimate property owner."

This was signed by three top Pottstown borough officials, and the great seal of the municipal corporation was pressed into it.

And no lawyer would take the municipality into court when citizens shrieked alarm about unjustified bills.

* * * * *

Until 1952, Pottstown borough constructed new streets at its own expense. Then the community grew so rapidly that the council felt it would go broke if it had to provide new streets for all the mushrooming housing developments.

The governing body then legislated to split the paving costs among abutting home owners and the borough. The property owner on each side of the street would pay one-third of the cost, the borough the final third.

This caused no great distress until some property owners began to get some borough bills for streets laid years before. They'd been guaranteed, they said, that the costs were to be borne by the borough. Who told them? The Veterans Administration, when veterans applied for loans.

* * * * *

There was no evidence of such a guarantee in city hall.

But Hill told this story in a Page-One display over multiple columns, on December 19, 1953:

"In the Philadelphia Veterans Administration office is a legal document which may explain why residents are balking at paying their share of street construction.

"The Veterans Administration document contains a guarantee that the borough will do the street paving at its own expense and shall levy no assessment upon the developer of the home or the ultimate property owner.

152

"The guarantee is signed by three Pottstown borough officials—two now out of office, but a third still retaining borough title.

"The only trouble with this guarantee . . . is that the clause was not on the original resolution passed by borough council May 9, 1949.

"Borough Hall minutes of council's meeting have no record of such a clause having been added to the original resolution which authorized the paving of streets in the northeast section of Pottstown.

"The codicil was believed to have been added after council had passed the paving resolution. The Veterans Administration appeared to be the only agency that has a copy of the 1949 resolution with the guarantee and the borough seal attached.

"There is no record at borough hall of council later having authorized such a guarantee.

"Your reporter sat with Veterans Administration officials in their spacious headquarters at 128 North Broad Street, Philadelphia, to discuss this unusual borough resolution. Long interviews were held with loan approval officials and finally with legal counsel.

"They refused to tell when the guarantee was added. There was no date attached to the 'afterthought' to indicate the time element.

"But there was indication in Pottstown that the original resolution, which did not provide funds for the construction of streets, did not meet Veterans Administration requirements. If veterans were to obtain loans to buy houses through the VA, construction of the streets had to be guaranteed.

"So, according to reports, the VA turned back the original resolution. Somehow, without the legal sanction of borough council, the following clause was attached to the VA copy of the law:

" 'It is also understood and agreed that the borough will do the afore-mentioned work at its own expense and shall levy no assessment upon the developer of the home or the ultimate property owner.'

"This appeared to satisfy the VA. Loans were made to some veterans who purchased homes in the development. Some other veterans obtained Federal Housing Administration loans.

"Veterans officials said they took the document signed by three borough officials and stamped by the borough seal in good faith. They had no reason to doubt its validity, they said over and over."

*　*　*　*　*

The story recounted how residents of the building development refused to pay their one-third share of street paving as provided by subsequent legislation. They planned to take their case into court.

But they never did.

They never did because they said a Pottstown lawyer turned down the case after vehemently declaring they had a just claim. Why? He couldn't win the case, the homeowners gave as his reason.

A Philadelphia lawyer pounded a table to declare: "You have a just claim." But he could not practice in Montgomery County!

The Philadelphia Savings Fund Society, which had advanced mortgage money, said it was sympathetic to homeowners but could do nothing because it had not been billed for the work. The invoices went to the property owners.

Some property owners were advised to disregard the bills. The borough promptly levied liens against the homes. If there is no settlement, the claims will become payable when the property is transferred.

*　*　*　*　*

And what of the borough officials who provided the VA with this "guarantee"?

154

"If my name is on it, I guess I signed it," the president of the council answered laconically.

"But why?" was the next question.

"My memory is a little hazy now. I can't answer that," he replied.

Why didn't the property owners take the borough into court?

"We could not get a lawyer to take the case," they said.

Which proves, possibly, that you can't win from city hall every time. But it also proved good digging by newspapermen will end this sort of secret negotiation.

There was no evidence of similar deals while The Mercury stood guard.

Chapter 23

CAN'T WIN 'EM ALL

Not everyone agrees with the editor. No newspaper wins all its crusades. Sometimes campaigns seem to have so little effect on the public that an editor wonders: "Oh, what's the use?"

But perseverance will out, as in the case of Shandy Hill's 30-year campaign to merge Pottstown's two hospitals. Beginning in the late 1930's he argued that consolidation was the only logical way to improve health care and to economize.

There were two hospitals. The older was Pottstown Hospital, an allopathic institution; the other was Homeopathic Hospital, which, as its name implies, was homeopathic. These differences mean nothing now, but they were a barrier then.

The editorial campaign generated some heat and some acceptance in hospital circles. Hill always felt most opposition came from the physicians. They had their little dynasties, and weren't willing to give them up.

The argument won some friends. The Pottstown Hospital directors were willing to merge, but an impasse resulted when the Homeopathic trustees voted. Even the result of the vote was challenged, for the proponents of merger were charged with skullduggery in obtaining a favorable vote by telephone, contrary to the bylaws.

So intense became the struggle that seven Homeopathic "anti-merger" directors took seven "pro-merger" trustees into court in 1942. The antis, accusing the mergerites of "a misguided spirit of public duty and . . . an erroneous belief in the efficacy of 'bigness,' " filed suit in 1942 seeking an injunction against continuation of the consolidation action.

The plaintiffs underwent a change of mind a little over a

156

week later, and the suit suddenly was withdrawn, three days before the court was to have heard argument. But disagreement never seemed to wane. If the hospital trustees were not battling for their positions, the medical staffs were declaring that "never the twain shall meet."

The Mercury editorial writer never let up. A more-than-30-year struggle ended in 1966, when the merged Pottstown Memorial Medical Center officially came into existence.

*   *   *   *   *

Not so victorious was The Mercury in another merger campaign. This one had to do with the public schools. It was suggested by The Mercury that the school districts in three contiguous townships merge with the larger Pottstown borough district, for economy reasons.

Merger was in the air then, and the State Department of Public Instruction was ordering consolidations, armed at providing better education.

Most officials of the two townships vigorously opposed merger with Pottstown, even though it was pointed out that duplication of buildings, equipment and teaching staffs would be eliminated. Provincialism won.

The Mercury had no way to gauge public sentiment, but it felt the man on the street favored merger. So, a poll of citizens was decided upon.

The Mercury planned to distribute straw ballots to every home, and to have the votes collected by newspaper carriers. The expense was to have been borne by the paper. Ballots were printed, ready for distribution, when the school boards in the three townships met in an unannounced session and voted to merge their three districts excluding Pottstown borough.

The vote was upheld by the state.

Chapter 24

FLINGS AT THE WHITE HOUSE

Time was, and not in the too-distant past, when small-town newspaper editors were so preoccupied with local problems, and their editorial rooms so understaffed, that they rarely wandered farther than the boundaries of their hometowns.

But the end of the war, the annihilation of space, which made distance no longer a problem, and better times not only gave the editor more time to think, but to exchange ideas with his peers.

There also was a disposition in Washington to open the government and its bureaus to all newspaper-comers, especially to invite the editor to the White House, to the Pentagon and to the Department of State. The editors were taken behind the scenes, briefed on what was to come in the rocket and space race (without direct attribution), and entertained socially by Presidents and their wives at the White House.

The American Society of Newspaper Editors provided the launching pad for this entry into the hush-hush land of government. As early as 1947, President Harry S. Truman invited the ASNE to a White House conference. But it was not an adequate confrontation; the conference room was too small and crowded.

Michael J. Ogden, editor of the Providence, R.I., Journal and Bulletin, described a Truman conference in 1961 when he was speaking before the ASNE. He said:

"I only attended one Presidential press conference, and that was under Truman, in the White House office in the old days. I found no one was inclined to let me be very far forward. I was in the back. I scarcely heard anything and I didn't see anything at all. At the end, one of our Washington bureau men took me up and introduced me to Mr. Truman.

158

He said: 'How is everything in Rhode Island?' I said, 'Very fine.' "

All this changed when John F. Kennedy was President. He threw open the White House to editors and their wives, declaring it "belonged to America." The practice was continued with éclat by Lyndon Baines Johnson.

The American Society of Newspaper Editors was honored by the appearance of the Presidents of the United States beginning with Herbert C. Hoover, in 1930. Highest men in government, as well as heads of foreign governments, accepted invitations to address the editors. Most controversial might have been Dr. Fidel Castro, of Cuba, who came to Washington in 1959, without the blessing of the State Department, but with a large contingent of his heavily-bearded fatigue-uniformed guards. He spoke for two hours and fifteen minutes.

But the appearance of Presidents and other dignitaries at society dinners gave little opportunity for the editors to get to know them personally. Some camaraderie might have been attained at ASNE "Bloody Mary" breakfasts given by the National Press Club, often attended by Supreme Court justices, cabinet members, heads of government agencies, Senators and military brass. There, the editor might press the hand of a politician while pressing for an answer to a question. But the field was too crowded and the time too limited for satisfaction.

*   *   *   *   *

President Kennedy addressed the ASNE in 1961—"a worried young man, slightly in need of a haircut," as Shandy Hill put it in a column in The Mercury, dwelling on the Cuban crisis.

His talk was not as surprising as a speech in 1963 when he concluded by inviting everybody to a White House reception that evening.

It was the first time in history that editors and their wives had been asked to a formal reception there.

The reception was on the second floor of the White House. The visitors had plenty of time to browse in the rooms. There was fruit punch (no alcohol) and dainty one-bite sandwiches. The U.S. Marine Corps orchestra played soft music in the foyer.

The President had been detained by business, but when he finally made his entrance from a side door, he had no opportunity to form a receiving line. The women who accompanied the editors actually mobbed him. They crushed the handsome, smiling chief executive against a wall, while he tried to greet as many as possible. The men waited for a long time before they could get to the President's side. Then they said their hello and goodbye and left the White House early.

Within a few months, the President had been cut down by an assassin's bullet. Hill was on a vacation freighter cruise at the time. His ship had docked at Georgetown, Barbados, that fateful November 22, 1963. Local newsmen came aboard to interview him about President Kennedy.

*   *   *   *   *

President Johnson continued the practice of entertaining the ASNE and wives at a White House reception. His first, on April 17, 1964, was quite a contrast to the quiet, formal party given by President Kennedy.

Hill reported in his column, "It was one of the folksiest parties in the sedate house of the Presidency. It was also one of the hardest to turn off. Editors filled the formal rooms of the White House to participate in the swinging dancing party that lasted after what many thought was beyond propriety."

Members of the society had been asked at noon that day to leave the White House around 7 P.M., and certainly not later than 7:30, because the President and Mrs. Johnson were entertaining other guests that night.

But the "folksy" atmosphere kept many there longer. Five bars and twelve buffet tables had been set up on the second floor of the White House. Hill reported, "Next to a Texas barbecue, this was the greatest."

An orchestra played in one of the White House wings and the guests danced under a huge many-tiered chandelier. President Johnson, known for his addiction to dancing, wanted to whirl with all the women. Since almost 400 women were there, he had set himself quite a goal. He didn't quite make it!

Some guests prepared to leave at 7, and at 7:30, ASNE President Michael Ogden strode to a microphone to thank President and Mrs. Johnson for a nice time. But nobody went home! At 7:45, the President led Mrs. Johnson onto the dance floor to the tune of "Good Night, Ladies."

It was a signal disregarded by some. Mrs. Martin S. Ochs, wife of the editor of the Chattanooga Times, was reported to have complained that the President had failed to dance with her. The President said, "We'll fix that. Strike up the band."

At 8, when the President was saying goodbye to guests, Mrs. James O. Powell, wife of the editor of the Little Rock, Ark., Gazette, complained, "I didn't dance with you, Mr. President." The President said, "We'll dance right here," and they did, without music.

Shortly after that, the party ended!

* * * * *

The next day, President Johnson made his first television appearance outside the White House and before a large audience in the Department of State auditorium. It was quite unlike the early Truman conferences. All editors were invited, and the hundreds of seats were filled by Washington correspondents and the visiting editors.

Mr. Johnson was said to have worried about how he looked before so large a crowd, but he made a remarkable appearance. At the end of the conference, he picked out a friend of long standing, John Quincy Mahaffey, of the Texarkana, Tex., Gazette, and asked him to accompany him in his drive back to the White House.

Mahaffey later reported the President hardly could wait to get into his automobile to inquire, "How did I do?"

President Johnson's White House receptions were slightly more restrained in succeeding years. In 1965, the "Texas barbecue" atmosphere was absent. Instead of the tables groaning under the weight of roast beef, baked ham and other impressive dishes, the food was more delicate. The sandwiches were dainty, and few two-fisted drinkers roamed the hallways.

The President and his daughter, Lynda Bird, were at the head of a receiving line, while Mrs. Johnson roamed through the rooms greeting friends. In addition, Vice President and Mrs. Hubert H. Humphrey mingled with guests in one of the wings. Cabinet officers took up conversational posts in other rooms.

The ASNE met in Montreal in 1966, and in 1968. President Johnson attended a summit meeting in Hawaii during the editors convention in Washington. But Mrs. Johnson received the guests at the White House, assisted by Vice President Humphrey.

*   *   *   *   *

Hill thought he had missed a story after his 1967 visit to the White House. At the very moment he arrived at the head of the receiving line, President Johnson was called into another room. He had been asked to say hello to Henry Belk, blind editor of the Goldsboro, N.C., News-Argus.

Lynda Johnson cautioned the visitors, "Please keep your positions in line, Daddy will be back in a few minutes."

While there, Hill made small talk with the President's daughter. He noticed her motioning to a tall, handsome White House aide in uniform.

"Let's go to a movie after this," she suggested.

This made little impression on Hill until the announcement of Lynda's engagement to the handsome Captain Charles S. Robb, a White House aide. Perhaps this exchange during the White House reception had been the beginning of their romance!

162

The more Hill thought about it, the more curious he became. So he did what any good reporter would do. He asked Mrs. Robb about it. Then employed by McCall's magazine, she was a good reporter too. She wrote:

"I wish I could put your mind to rest, but I can't remember if the military aide to whom you refer was indeed Captain Robb. I guess it will just have to remain a mystery—a hard thing for any good reporter to accept!"

*   *   *   *   *

Mike Ogden's eight-word conversation with President Truman reminded Hill of a brief encounter he had with the sharp-tongued Truman after the chief executive retired from office.

Hill was in Washington for a Department of State briefing and stopped at the Mayflower Hotel. An early riser, Hill took a walk, then went to the hotel newsstand to buy a newspaper.

An inveterate early riser-walker, ex-President Truman was at the newsstand too, obviously waiting for the breakfast room's 7 A.M. opening. He was with a male companion, probably a secret service guard.

Looking up, Hill greeted the President with a cheery "Good morning, Mister President."

Truman replied quickly, "Good morning! How are you?"

Hill, engrossed now in the newspaper headlines, casually answered, "I'm well, thank you."

There was an embarrassing pause. Something was lacking. Then the ex-President supplied it.

"Well, I'm well, too," he said tartly and strode into the breakfast room.

*   *   *   *   *

Vice President Hubert H. Humphrey was in the receiving line when the American Society of Newspaper Editors was entertained there in April, 1968. He stood to the left of Mrs.

163

Lyndon B. Johnson. President Johnson was in Hawaii on a Vietnam war conference.

After being greeted by Mrs. Johnson with the usual small talk, Shandy Hill firmly grasped the hand of Humphrey and looked deep into his twinkling eyes.

"When you come to Pennsylvania, we will take care of you," Hill told the vice president. He was referring to the 1968 election.

"Thank you! Thank you!", the vice president replied.

The chance remark Hill made turned out to be prophetic. For, in the Democratic party national convention in Chicago that year, Pennsylvania's vote assured the vice president of the presidential nomination. The convention didn't have to go beyond the P's. Pennsylvania put him over.

Then, in the November general election, Pennsylvania voted Democratic to give Humphrey one of the few states in his column.

Vice President Humphrey recalled the prophecy.

"When you told me that Pennsylvania would take care of me, you were so right," he wrote Hill after the presidential election. "My visits to the state were good ones, the state stood with me at the national convention, and Pennsylvania's electoral votes gave us much hope on election night."

Then he lightly touched on his "retirement" by the electorate with this comment: "I hope I enjoy my retirement as much as you seem to be."

Chapter 25

PURELY LOCAL

Members of the newspaper profession called The Mercury's approach to Page One "unique" and "novel." Nothing but local news and local pictures was used on the first page. National and world news was not neglected, but it was emphasized on the first page of the second section, or inside the paper. News of the world always was published completely, even up to the point of remaking press at the last minute. But local news was the chief commodity The Mercury sold.

This "unique" approach was a magnet that attracted readers. Leo Riordan, formerly an editor of The Philadelphia Inquirer and later director of public relations at a Philadelphia hospital, wrote Shandy Hill about "your novel approach to Page One."

Riordan continued:

"It is in direct contrast to the unfortunate policy that is growing upon some big city papers of just grabbing Associated Press or United Press International copy and shoveling it into the composing room.

"Your first-page approach is not easy, but it must be very effective with your readers. Too many papers across the country are like too many other papers, without individualism. The same comics, the same columns, the same wire stories do not give readers the feeling of being personally involved."

The "approach" wasn't new. It was as old as the first newspaper, Hill reminded members of the Pennsylvania Associated Press Managing Editors Association, when he was invited to speak by Joseph H. Snyder, state manager.

A hundred years before, Horace Greeley in 1861 had advised: "The subject of deepest interest to the average

165

GROUND-TURNING for a State highway in Pottstown, Pa., was done by Shandy Hill after years of promoting a bypass. Governor William W. Scranton, of Pennsylvania, who is directly behind Hill, made the dedicatory address.

human being is himself. Next to that, he is most concerned about his neighbors. Asia and Tonga islands stand a long way after these in his regard."

Greeley didn't suggest neglect of news from afar, but he said that unless the editor could convince the reader his local ideas were worth reading, he was not going to create much interest in his long-distance observation.

Charles A. Dana, the great New York Sun editor, put it another way. "A tomcat on the steps of city hall is more important than a crisis in the Balkans," he said.

Hill also quoted some other big-city editors who had the small-town idea that local news is what makes the paper. John Chapman, in his book, "Tell It To Sweeney," said about the largest daily newspaper in the United States in 1920, "Local stories, colorful and exciting were breaking and The New York Daily News was learning how to play them. A good local story held more news and mass reader interest than most national or international developments."

*   *   *   *   *

That was the assessment of the editors of a paper with two million circulation daily and three million on Sundays. Could a 25,000 circulation paper do otherwise?

Basil L. "Stuffy" Walters, who retired as executive editor of The Chicago Daily News in 1961, after great success there, said that when he first took over the Chicago job, "The news might as well have been produced in San Francisco, Dallas or Albany."

On the day he went to Chicago, Walters said, he found his entire edition of The Daily News contained only one local story. His greatest achievement was to bring the paper in balance. He made a far better local paper, far more service-able to the people living in and near Chicago.

There was a time when every night a news service sent out a budget, showing just what The New York Times was pub-lishing on Page One. Many papers then decided to ape The

—Courtesy, Easton Express

POLITICALLY the Pottstown Mercury was independent, but political news always found a top spot. Editor Shandy Hill "made" news when he arranged the first political debate between Pennsylvania congressional candidates in 1968. When television was trying to arrange a "confrontation" between Senator Joseph S. Clark and Congressman Richard S. Schweiker, Hill scooped them by arranging a debate for the annual meeting of the Pennsylvania Associated Press Managing Editors Association. Here are the "combatants": left to right, Mrs. and Senator Clark; Hill; Congressman and Mrs. Schweiker.

Times. It led to newspapermen's caustic criticism that many editors edited their newspapers for the benefit of nearby editors. Hill decided The Mercury could be aggressive, interesting and even more reliable and better edited than its big neighbors.

Its big neighbors were the Philadelphia Evening Bulletin, one of the largest evening papers, and The Philadelphia Inquirer, only 40 miles away, both with wide circulation in the Pottstown area; The Reading Times and The Reading Eagle, seventeen miles distant, hemming in The Mercury to the west, and the Allentown Call to the north, with 88,000 circulation.

So the Mercury had to give Pottstown something the metropolitans could not—local news—or suffer the stodgy fate of most small-town newspapers, which were unimpressive and weak, resembling throwaways. If The Mercury were to succeed in providing a lively, complete newspaper, it would have to be different from "too many other papers, without individualism," as Riorden had pointed out.

*   *   *   *   *

The Mercury had to offer something more than news which the people already had heard on radio and seen on television. This something had to be exclusive, something to leave the reader with a feeling that he had received his money's worth. This was exclusive news, and often the reader said there was "too much in the paper"—he couldn't read it all.

The Mercury delayed its deadlines so it might give later news than the metropolitans. Frequently it "made over" inside or telegraph pages to insert latest news associations bulletins, and then told its public: "You find it only in The Mercury." The reader really didn't need to be reminded about this. He generously boasted it was the best small-town paper in the country!

That The Mercury succeeded in providing a lively, complete newspaper was shown in public acceptance, and, after all, a newspaper is good only when its public so describes it. The Mercury's circulation rose steadily, until in 1957 its circulation was greater than the borough's population, reaching a daily net paid figure of 23,743 in a less-than-22,000 population town. This in itself was unique, for that year only ten other dailies of the 1,800 in the United States, could boast greater circulations than their city populations.

Content meant nothing if it was not well written and if it did not cover the field. The Mercury met both requirements and in so doing, developed public involvement. Hardly a month went by that The Mercury was not involving people in the news, getting them to express their opinions, getting them to help their neighbor or the less fortunate, mobilizing them against unsound government or to war against intolerance or to challenge those who would infringe on the public's right to know. The Mercury became strong because it had more than good writing; it knew what was in the hearts of its readers.

This feeling of pride in their newspaper often was displayed by vacationers, who came back to Pottstown with newspapers they picked up from cities along their way.

"Just look at this," they would point out, "it doesn't come close to The Mercury."

*   *   *   *   *

Professional journalists were quick to recognize it wasn't an easy task to produce a newspaper dedicated to the public service, yet presenting the news so completely that it was an accurate reflection of the life of the community. Publishing such a newspaper involved the creative work of an alert and diligent staff, guided by a dedicated leader who wouldn't allow the paper to be edited from the counting room.

How to keep a staff stimulated to the demands of production, which included quality, diversity and interest, was not always easy. But the real newspaper people on the staff enjoyed the rewards of doing a good job and of being so big a part of a good newspaper.

Staffers "lived" their stories. They were given some outrageous assignments, yet they wrote engrossing feature stories after riding in a coffin to a cemetery, becoming surgeons or bakers for a day, walking miles through sewer networks for a Jean Valjean experience, exposing fortune tellers and "seers," writing and taking pictures of slot-machine and pinball gambling, playing Santa Claus in department stores, and ringing the Christmas bell for the Salvation Army at its kettles.

Wide and varied was the range of these demands, particularly when the circus was in town. Hill was a circus buff. He was a close acquaintance of the glamorous press agents of the circus, ate with them, drank with them and concocted "stunts" to stimulate reader interest, as well as attendance at the performances.

The Mercury always had a staffer in the circus. This was no new "stunt," for newspapers did it everywhere, but the reader "ate it up." Especially when a local reporter rode as a clown in the street parade atop an elephant, or girl reporters ate with the women performers and wrote of their spectacular lives.

* * * * *

What might have been the most memorable of these "stunts" (Hill never was able to convince a staffer he ought to assist Clyde Beattie in the animal cage) was the appearance of a Mercury reporter in a flying trapeze act. A hundred feet at tenttop, he sailed toward the waiting grasp of the catchers while thousands of breathless patrons below were hushed.

This daring young man on the flying trapeze was William F. Achatz, now Pennsylvania state picture editor of the Associated Press.

It was in the mid-1930s and the circus was Hagenback-Wallace, then one of the largest three-ring circuses in the world. The bigtop seated 5,000, a capacity that not even the most optimistic of press agents expected in a small town of 20,000. But The Mercury and Billy Achatz accomplished that feat.

In a conversation with an advance man, Hill had suggested that a reporter be permitted to join the Flying Wallendas, a daring trio of flying trapeze artists. There were two men and one woman, wife of a "flier."

Hill told the public relations man he had just the right man to do the stunt, a staffer with courage, unafraid of heights because he was a professional parachute jumper on weekends! Hill overrode objections because of the danger, then got permission from the circus management.

Achatz readily agreed to "join" the circus. He was to have exactly one day of practice to "perfect" his role of flier. So the day before the Pottstown performance, he went to a nearby city to "practice" with the professionals.

The day of the Pottstown performance saw the bigtop filled to capacity. To a burst of applause, Achatz appeared, all decked out in white, with puffy tights, long hose, low-cut jersey and white shoes. He followed the professionals to the launching platform, high above a rope net. The catcher swung out from the opposite side of the tent, looped the back of his knees around the trapeze bar, and swooped down in a gesture of "Let's go, I'm ready to play catch."

The Mercury's photographer also was ready to record this event for history!

Achatz swung out in a graceful parabola. He released himself from the trapeze, reaching for the catcher's outstretched arms, and missed!

The crowd gasped.

He dropped to the rough net below, landed on his back, then arose and took giant, ungraceful leaps to the aerialists' ladder once more.

He climbed to the platform, and the catcher's rhythmic swinging and an empty trapeze started once more. Then

172

Achatz grabbed the bar, and waited for the command "Go." He swung far out to the center of the tent, reached for the catcher's arms and fell once more!

Hill stopped the act. He asked Achatz to give up, and the capacity crowd understood. Applause was unrestrained, and The Mercury sold well the next morning as it depicted, in prose and picture, the daring young man's adventure.

*　*　*　*　*

The Mercury "localized" everything. When President Kennedy was victim of an aching back, Pottstown folk were invited to tell how they suffered from lower lumbar region trouble, and how they eased the pain.

When an earthquake occurred in San Francisco, The Mercury telephoned a Californian for an eye-witness report. Florida hurricanes became localized when Mercury subscribers were called to recount their experiences and describe the damage.

When a disaster occurred, The Mercury asked, "Can It Happen Here?" and explained whether it could!

Everything was local! If one's own name was the sweetest-sounding word in the English language, Mercury readers heard it often. Many a small-town person gets three newspaper mentions in his lifetime—birth, marriage and death. The Mercury's 100,000 readers could expect publication of their names at least once a year, and that's no exaggeration. They were featured in long birthday lists, wedding anniversaries, "personals" and the like. Nothing was too small to escape The Mercury's attention; no person was too insignificant for attention.

The Mercury was the haven for the troubled, and the harbor for those adrift on the seas of despair. People turned to it first for all sorts of reasons, but mostly because they felt pride in it. They telephoned in before calling fire companies when their houses were afire; they called or dropped in after accidents, before they reported to police, they reported all their joys and woes.

Those wanting favors, naturally, beat a path to the editor's door. Politicians, those in office and those aspiring to office, sought the editor's advice. Those with opinions contrary to the newspaper's didn't hesitate to "rouse" the editor, because he always was in reach of the telephone.

No wonder, then, that the newspaper became a vital part of Pottstonians' lives. Some detractors vilified it, but these were the same persons who could not wait until the next morning to pick it up from their doorsteps. The Mercury, with the school and the pulpit, helped Pottstown attain a high level of citizenship.

With all this, the reader sought leadership, and The Mercury provided this without being swayed by friendship or fear of foe. There was some doubt at first, some notions of search for power, but the readers soon learned The Mercury would take positive stands with a clear conviction that its position was best for the public's interest. It wasn't necessary for The Mercury to be right always, just so long as it didn't straddle the fence. The reader, when aroused, often responded by "throwing out the rascals" at the ballot box.

Chapter 26

CRITICS ALWAYS PRESENT

The small-town newspaper editor is always on the firing line. He has no receptionist to screen visitors. The irate subscriber with pet peeves, and the do-gooder with pet projects, walk into the office, confront the editor and get a hearing. There is no escaping them.

The telephone operators learn to know the voices of the "nuts" of the community, and sometimes are able to delay or sidetrack inquiries about service or nitpicking whines about petty inaccuracies.

But many of these calls will get through because if the editor is conscientious, he wants to know what the community is thinking about. Some of the screwiest complaints may lead to stories.

In a small town, the editor is harassed by the inevitable ill feeling generated by his fighting newspaper. There are doubts and suspicions. He is accused of seeking power, possibly with political maneuvering. If the editor is to achieve in part his aim of publishing the news without fear or favor, he must shake off suspicion, but remain alert to it. He lives in a business where he gives; he must learn to take.

*　　*　　*　　*　　*

Shandy Hill's role was no more rugged than those of other crusading editors. His name was synonymous with The Mercury. He was the butt of all charges, many of them imagined. He was the executioner, and the executioner is never popular. But then Hill often said he was not running a popularity contest.

The Mercury gave identity to the community. It reflected Hill's personality, his character, his toughness, pugnacity,

175

kindness, humor and compassion. It made the community. The Mercury was a living thing that reflected the personality of the man who lived, ate and slept newspaper.

Hill took many of the petty irritations in stride. There was the usual number of the "Dear Sir, You Cur" letters. Anonymous for the most part, many could be recognized as products of the poison-pen disease, a common mental aberration that afflicts persons otherwise perfectly normal.

The poison-pen communications come with astonishing regularity. They follow a pattern so definite that the target knows when to look for them.

Let there be an editorial on a controversial issue, and the editor could expect the vilest slander, to the point of ugly repetition. The more the authors feel thwarted in their goal of hurting the editor, the more the slander is reiterated.

* * * * *

Every Thursday morning, week after week, year after year, a neatly printed postcard containing Biblical quotations, was addressed personally to the editor, obviously meant to strike terror into the editor's calloused heart. "Woe to them when they write injustices" (Isaiah 10:1), the writer would proclaim; "Being filled with all iniquity; malice, fornication, avarice, full of envy, murder, contention, deceit" (Romans 1:29); or "For thou writest bitter things against me" (Job 13:16), or "For the wages of sin is death," (Romans 6:23).

The search every Thursday morning became a game. "Wonder what he'll say today," staffers speculated. Hill was a little proud of this attention, but pride melted when he learned he wasn't alone as a target of castigation. He learned that Msgr. William M. Begley, pastor of a Roman Catholic parish, the Rev. Wallace Flood, a Baptist and the Rev. Donald A. Ottinger, a Methodist, were receiving identical postcards every week. The thrill evaporated!

Hill felt a little worry for the perpetrator when the Pottstown postmaster passed the word that postal investigators had looked into the mailings. The investigators knew the name of the writer, where the postcards were mailed every week, and the persons who were receiving them. Like some other human pleasures, when the hidden was exposed, the anticipation lost its appeal.

Saddest part of all was that the mailings stopped when Hill left the newspaper, as though his retirement had expiated all sins and no further gospel guidance was needed by the sinner!

Another postcard fan, a hate slinger, wrote frequently about the editor's alleged addiction to Mt. Vernon rye whisky. Hill was pleased to be recognized as a connoisseur, for Mt. Vernon was high priced in the middle of the 1940's.

*   *   *   *   *

Hill's sympathy went out to the poor warped souls who imagined the newspaper was "writing things" about them. One classic example was a woman who charged that Dr. George W. Crane, a psychologist and physician with a syndicated daily advice column, was making her a direct butt of his writings. What's more and what was harder to take, she was sure Hill himself was writing the column.

This wasn't unusual, for many in Pottstown believed and actually asserted that Hill wrote everything in the paper. They could not be convinced that a staff took care of this, that he didn't work around the clock.

This distraught woman accosted Hill on the street, then became an early-morning caller at the office. She appeared in her nightclothes, wrapped in a housecoat. She wore bedroom slippers. She demanded to see the editor, and would speak only to the editor.

Some employees, who quickly learned to recognize her, would make excuses. "Mr. Hill won't be in until late this afternoon," they would tell her. But she would reply, "All right, I'll wait," and take a chair in the lobby.

Hill tried all sorts of dodges to avoid her. He would hide in an advertising cranny, or sneak under counters, but she would wait. And soon it devolved on Hill to see her, sympathize with her, calm her down, assure her Dr. Crane didn't mean her and then get her to drive home. Hill feared someone in her distressed state of mind might get into an accident. He often had employees shadow her to see no harm came her way.

She would be back in a couple of days. Convinced that Hill was making millions of dollars writing about her, she demanded a part of the profit.

"You are a millionaire, aren't you?" she would ask, as if what newspaperman wasn't?

Evidently things got rough at her home, and she finally reproached her husband about the Crane columns. He came in to see Hill, and asked, "What can I do about this woman?" Hill showed him the envelopes and copy. The husband said maybe his best bet was to drive her to Mellott, Indiana, to see Dr. Crane or establish that the column copy was not produced in Pottstown. This suggestion ended the chapter.

Dr. Crane was not immune to this sort of harassment.

"A woman at Akron (Ohio)," he told Hill, "was a twin for the lady you mentioned, for she charged me with invading her privacy and writing her personal case, though I had never seen or heard of her. I employ pseudonyms for these patients whom I use as cases."

* * * * *

Loud threats never worry a newspaperman. It's the sneaky kind that irritate.

Shandy Hill was frightened only once by complainers—and this was a woman!

A baby had swallowed strychnine tablets and died. The toddler had pulled off a tablecloth, and found the pills. A Mercury editorial said anyone who carelessly placed poison within reach of youngsters was courting disaster.

Many days after this editorial—and it already was forgotten—a neatly dressed, handsome woman came into The

178

Mercury office and asked to see Mr. Hill. She carried a large handbag, large enough almost to be a satchel. She asked to see Mr. Hill privately, where no one could see or hear.

Seldom was such a request granted. Hill, always a shirt-sleeved newspaperman, sat out in the open editorial room to grant interviews. But the woman insisted, and Hill took her into a closed office. She sat across the desk from Hill, placing the huge handbag on the floor beside her chair, out of Hill's sight.

"I am the mother of the boy you said I killed," she began. It took Hill a little time to link the editorial with the boy's death and the handsome woman, but when he did, he became apprehensive.

After tearfully reciting a long story of her grief and how beautiful her child had been, she reached into her bag and said, "I want to show you something."

Hill evidently was edgy that morning. "Oh, oh! Here it comes," he mused. "This is the time for the gun!"

The woman brought up a framed colored photograph. "This is a picture of my dead son." she cried. "Isn't he handsome?" Hill agreed.

Then the woman reached to the floor again. "Now it's coming." Hill told himself. "The gun's coming!"

The woman came up with a pair of baby shoes. She gently placed them on the desk and lamented, "This is all I have left!"

It took some doing to pacify this visitor, but Hill did it.

* * * * *

Everything comes to him who orders hash, and so does everything finally reach the editor's desk—including a sample of floor sweepings from a woman who declared the community was trying to poison her. Pottstown, she said, was polluting the air and this was killing her.

The editor gets accustomed to drunks who get him out of bed after the paper hits the streets to complain about some-

179

thing that didn't make the front pages or the sports pages.

"Say, how'd Joe Bish make out in that fight last night?" the anonymous caller would ask chidingly.

"Bish won the decision," Hill invariably would reply, only to be stunned by the resulting query: "What was the decision?"

Hill never got too angry with these boors, even though he was puzzled by one female's query. Obviously in a barroom—the juke box music was in the background, there was loud talking and her voice was thick—she courteously brayed, "Hey, Hill, what's a clam stem?"

Hill cut her off somehow, but there was no more sleeping for him that morning. Just what is a clam stem? He thought and thought. Suddenly the light flashed. In an editorial, he had written something about police desk sergeants having so little work that their main job was to run downtown at lunchtime to buy the chief a clam stew. And the word "stew" came up "stem"!

Not quite as bad as the unfortunate editor who threw himself into a gaudy editorial on the passing of a woman pillar of a church, only to have·the last line appear as: "Gone to her last roasting place."

* * * * *

One woman did cause an explosion in Hill's home one New Year's morning, when he was called out of bed by a notorious griper. He might have kept his temper had he not been up that New Year's morning until 5, celebrating the arrival of another year with a party in his kitchen. To go with the ginger ale, the partiers had been eating egg sandwiches on which reposed thick slices of Bermuda onion!

Onions have a soporific quality, and this probably was why Hill was able to fall asleep as soon as he trundled to his bedroom. No sooner had he fallen off to sleep when the telephone rang.

The clang was a call to disaster, he was certain.

180

Dashing out of bed, he half fell, half jumped down the stairs to hear the caller ask:

"Didn't you get out a paper this morning?"

"Yes ma'am, we did," he replied while a wisp of smoke curled out of his head. "Didn't you get yours?"

"No, I did not." the woman brusquely said, "and I want one."

Then Hill did something he never did before. He passed the buck.

"I don't have anything to do with delivery," he said, "but why don't you call Walter Zimmerman? He's our circulation manager. He'll see you get one. His number is 323-4699."

Hill hung up the receiver and slowly crawled back to bed. Morpheus was good to him, and he dozed off immediately.

Again the phone rang. Again Hill responded like a fire horse. Again he slid down the stairs.

"Hello," said the voice of the same woman. "What did you say the number was?"

Chapter 27

DEAR SIR, YOU CUR

Everybody in small (population 25,000) Pottstown knew Shandy Hill, but Hill did not know all the 100,000 persons who made up the trading area. Many only thought they knew Hill; they knew the name that was synonymous with The Mercury and because the name was so well known, so often repeated, so controversial, they imagined they were acquainted with the name's owner.

They imagined more. They believed Hill wrote everything in the paper, working 24 hours a day. They charged him with its errors, but gave him sparing praise for what good he did. Some never learned that a newspaper doesn't make the news, it merely prints it.

People delight in being close to newspapermen. Tipsters revel in supplying news. Others hang around the newsroom all day, if allowed, hoping some of the glamor might rub off.

Another group is the "aggrieved," who build up hatreds because of some real or imagined hurt. They might have demanded, "Who gave you the right to print that story?" and gotten the stock reply that a newspaper needs no such permission. Their toes are trod on and never heal. So they harbor thoughts of revenge.

Embezzlers are never guilty! It's the newspaper's fault they've stolen money, because the newspaper reports it! Politicans always are misquoted! Somehow, a quotation in black and white seems different to them from the words they precipitously uttered.

So there's many a chance for nuts and poison-pen writers to make a whipping boy out of the editor. But editors learn to dish it out, and they can take it.

Likewise, there's many an opportunity for persons who

don't even know the editor to castigate him, to pretend they have the goods on the editorial writer!

*   *   *   *   *

John Quincy Mahaffey, Texarkana, Tex., Gazette editor, told about his woes in a short talk before the American Society of Newspaper Editors, and Hill wrote about it in his column in The Mercury. Said Mahaffey:

"I have more critics, I guess, than any other man in this room.

"The elderly and retired people of Texarkana say to one another in the early morning hours, 'We haven't got anything to do today, so let's go downtown and tell John Quincy Mahaffey how to run the Texarkana Gazette.'

"I will say that there are more assorted nuts and bores coming through the doors of city rooms clear across this nation than ever before in my 30 years of journalism. Some of these people really ought to be confined. I don't know what they are doing walking around the streets of our cities.

"I'm a great critic of the reading public. I think a big part of the reading public either can't read or they read too much into a story. I want to illustrate that point with a very old story that I have been telling for about thirty years.

"It's a story about a column I wrote about a big black dog named Blackie. Blackie and I were not friends. As a matter of fact, I hated his guts. He would leave old dinosaur bones and brassieres and corsets on my front lawn. And when I would shoo him out of my flowerbeds, he would stalk majestically out of the yard looking back over his shoulder as if to say, 'I'm leaving, but not because I'm afraid of you.'

"The column I wrote about Blackie had to do with his sudden disappearance. I said in the column that I was not fond of the old dog, but I did have a certain admiration for him because of his tremendous dignity and I hoped that somebody else had not taken a violent dislike to him and poisoned his food.

183

"Well, no sooner had our paper hit the steps of our stupid subscribers—when one of them got on the 'phone and said in a very sinister voice, 'I know who poisoned old Blackie; you did, you s.o.b.' "

* * * * *

Some who think they are harrying the editor with baseless charges are only eating out their insides. Hill not only enjoyed deflating stiff shirtfronts but he sometimes raucously and ill-manneredly brought the detractors to heel.

Scurrilous and ill-founded accusations often fill the "telephone talk" periods on the radio. These programs allow callers to pop off without rebuttal and worse yet, without divulging their identities.

Hill was considered fair game on such a show, and one woman, in particular, castigated him for the newspaper's errors and for evils she imagined. Probably hundreds in the area—including Hill—knew who the woman was, but she felt certain of her anonymity.

One afternoon, a small group of women met in The Mercury to welcome a politician seeking state office. The candidate's arrival was set back by delays in other cities, and the meeting was delayed from 2 to 4 P.M. Yet one matron, decked out in a flowered dress and an eye-opening hat, arrived at 2.

"You'll have a long wait," Hill told her. "The candidate won't be here until four."

"If you don't mind, I'll wait," said the woman.

"Not at all," replied Hill. "Come into the office. Make yourself comfortable," pushing a chair her way. "Did you read this morning's paper? No? Well, spend some time reading it," and he handed her a Mercury.

"By the way," he continued, "my name is Shandy Hill. And what is yours?"

She told him.

"Ah, you're the woman who's always on the radio cutting

184

me up!" Hill said with a smile, waiting for the knife to sink. But she met him with a poker face, although a bit of color faded from her cheeks.

"Oh, no," she lied. "You're wrong! Not I. You know, so many people have the same kind of voice I have!'"

* * * * *

Ted Drippe, proprietor of a Pottstown toy store, was doubled with laughter when he came into the office one afternoon.

"You should have been there," he told Hill. "You must have seen us talking when you parked your car."

There, indeed, had been a couple in the driveway, chatting animatedly. When Hill parked the car, he said hello to Drippe and walked out.

"Did you see that guy I was talking to? Know him?" Drippe asked the questions in one breath. The answers were "yes" and "no." He seemed shocked when Hill said he didn't know the man.

"Well, you should have been there," repeated the visitor. "For a half hour he's been telling me what a lousy newspaper The Mercury is, and what a monster that Shandy Hill is. Really took you over the coals."

"Do you know Shandy Hill very well?" Drippe had asked the man.

"Know him? Why I've known him for 30 years and I wouldn't be seen in his company. He's the most disliked man in Pottstown," continued the derogator, lacing his sentences with choice expletives.

"Just then you parked your car, walked out and greeted me," Drippe went on.

"As I watched you go out, the man turned to me and anxiously asked, 'Say, who's that fella?' I couldn't wait to ask, 'Don't you know him? That's Shandy Hill.' "

Exit Drippe, laughing.

185

Chapter 28

POTTSTOWN ON PARADE

"Pottstown on Parade," a slick little magazine, thumbnailed Shandy Hill in its Pottstown Bi-Centennial Issue of 1952.

Its feature writer, Larry Davis, drew a portrait under the title "Big Business is News." He wrote:

"Shandy Hill of The Mercury is perhaps Pottstown's most constant booster, and although hundreds of people meet him on the street in the course of a week, thousands more know him by name only.

"As pilot of The Mercury, Hill has injected his life and his personality into its pages so that today its circulation is well over 20,000, a phenomenal figure in light of the borough's near 25,000 population. His paper is 'must' reading at breakfast in almost 10,000 homes in the borough alone.

"A graduate of Lehigh University and a former Reading newspaperman and radio sports commentator, Hill is a strict disciplinarian, not only of his own work, but also of the policies that have elevated The Mercury to the top spot in first-class nationwise competition. Among his colleagues in the business, he is known as a newspaperman's newspaperman. And there is no higher tribute.

"Hill is the natural enemy of social regimentation and dictatorial cussedness. He is a champion of the underdog and a friend of those needing help. As a result, his stories and editorials, written in crisp staccato syllables that paint vivid word pictures, consistently have led the way for Pottstown's growth and expansion.

"The graying newsman, whose interest in his work has never dulled, seldom is to be found in his private office. Instead he beats a rattling typewriter in the paper's newsroom, close to the teletype and closer to the telephone, the people and the community to which he has given almost a quarter of a century. He has been known to pull on his weathered felt hat and seek out hot news as though his managerial duties were secondary.

"Politically, Hill is a non-partisan; he is concerned only with results. Consequentially, in its editorial column, The Mercury had been for and against both major parties.

"He has a tremendous capacity for work, a drawing energy that last year laid him flat on his back in a hospital. During World War II he refused to take a vacation; and besides his normal administrative and supervisory duties, he shouldered the assignments that his depleted staff could not possibly 'cover,' after completing his usual nine hour day.

"Hill's news columns are open to any worthwhile cause that will promote Pottstown or that will improve its political, civic, social or economic status; and he has devoted miles of 'copy' to the interest of charity.

"For his entire career, Shandy Hill has never faltered in his drive to make Pottstown a better community in which to live."

* * * * *

The Bell Telephone Company of Pennsylvania mixed flowers and barbs in a salute to Shandy Hill in the Pennsylvania Newspaper Publishers' Association Press Bulletin in August, 1962.

With a picture of Hill seated at his desk, a vase of roses prominent in the foreground, The Bell Telephone Company said in a "We salute . . ." feature in the magazine:

"The pages of The Pottstown Mercury have much in common with roses on Shandy Hill's desk. They are something to be anticipated and enjoyed. And, as good roses and good newspapers should, they also have thorns.

"The Mercury's character as a keen observer of and commentator on the local scene reflects the influence of the

187

ROSES AND THORNS is the way the Bell Telephone Company of Pennsylvania put it when it published this "Salute" to Shandy Hill in the Pennsylvania Newspaper Publishers' "Press Bulletin" in 1962.

general manager and staff, who are prompt and unstinting in praising what is good for Pottstown and tireless in opposing what is not.

"Shandy Hill's 30 years with The Mercury have brought him many honors and even a few offers of tar and feathers. Both are to be expected when public service is the driving force behind your efforts."

EPILOGUE

The Mercury was sold by William M. Hiester on December 23, 1966, to Ralph M. Ingersoll, former New York publisher, and TV producers Mark Goodson and William Todman.

Shandy Hill retired in July, 1967.